# Carved out of the Rock

# Carved out of the Rock

By

Greta MacDonald

Carved out of the Rock
By
Greta MacDonald



Published by Emmanuel Christian Centre
Irvine
KA12 8RD
Scotland

Third edition June 2016

First printing December 2008



Published by Campaign Literature
3 Nineyard Street, KA21 5HS

# Dedication

First, to my Lord and Saviour, whose love and faithfulness have been with me through all the journey of life, and who constrained me to write this book, so that others may read and be encouraged. He is who He says He is in His eternal Word - the One who cannot fail.

Second, to the memory of my partner in the work, Duncan, now in the Glory, waiting on the re-union with the saints on that glorious day.

"Before and after"

Men at work

# Foreword

I have been privileged to know and fellowship with Greta and her husband over many years. Duncan is now with Jesus in Heaven having departed this life following years of dedicated Christian service and ministry.

Duncan and Greta laboured together in the cause of the Gospel. Both were visionaries, building their ministries around the early church record in the book of Acts of the first century apostles. I crusaded with them on a number of occasions, witnessing the conversions, healings and deliverances comparable with those in the early church.

The first services were convened in the Volunteer Rooms and later in the Conservative Halls in the centre of Irvine, Scotland.

Duncan, who worked in the technical department of a High School, was the ideal person to renovate and refurbish their present church building in West Road, Irvine.

Upon completion, the new venue has become the centre for renewal and revival. It is a lighthouse of hope for those in spiritual darkness, a healing centre for the suffering and a venue for renewal and restoration.

Christ Jesus is uplifted in worship and praise. The pure word of God is faithfully proclaimed and an ongoing welcome awaits all who visit with their problems and needs.

I'm certain this record of God's faithfulness over the years will stimulate your faith, inspire your vision and cause you to render praise and glory to God for the dedicated servants Duncan and Greta MacDonald and their loyal team members.

Rev Peter Scothern
New Testament Ministries

1983—"Through the double doors were the roof lights"

# Preface

This story has been written to put on record the great works of God, enlightening those who follow to know and appreciate the vision of the Emmanuel Christian Centre. This vision has always been, and will always be, the Lord's doing and it is marvellous in our eyes.

If this book makes any positive contribution to the reader's understanding of faith in the Living God, I will have good reason for giving thanks to Him who guided my pen to write.

Greta MacDonald
Irvine
Scotland
14 April 2008

Weekends away

Fun & fellowship

# Acknowledgements

I am most grateful to the team members, adherents of the Fellowship and friends, who stood by both Duncan and me for the past twenty years, and who have also continued to support me personally over the past four years. Their prayers and sacrifice have not gone unnoticed. There are some who stand out, namely:

Billy, Lilian, Ellis, Margaret, Thor, Wendy and Ann

Many others could be named who joined later, whose ministry has been invaluable, and I express here my warmest appreciation for their love, loyalty and giftings to the body of Christ, which is the Church. One of these is Bernie, who 'caretakes' and keeps the House of God clean.

Next, a big "Thank you" to my many personal friends, among whom is Pastor Bridie Watters, Gina Cooke, Ruth Stirling, Margaret Jones and my niece Jacqueline, who love me unconditionally and support me in the ministry.

Last but not least to Billy Aitken MBE, who supported Duncan and me in the administration side of the work for about 20 years, his input has been invaluable.

Also a very special "Thank you" to my much loved daughter, Elaine, who understands when I need to talk, she is always there for me.

Pastor Greta

What the old church looked like when we bought it

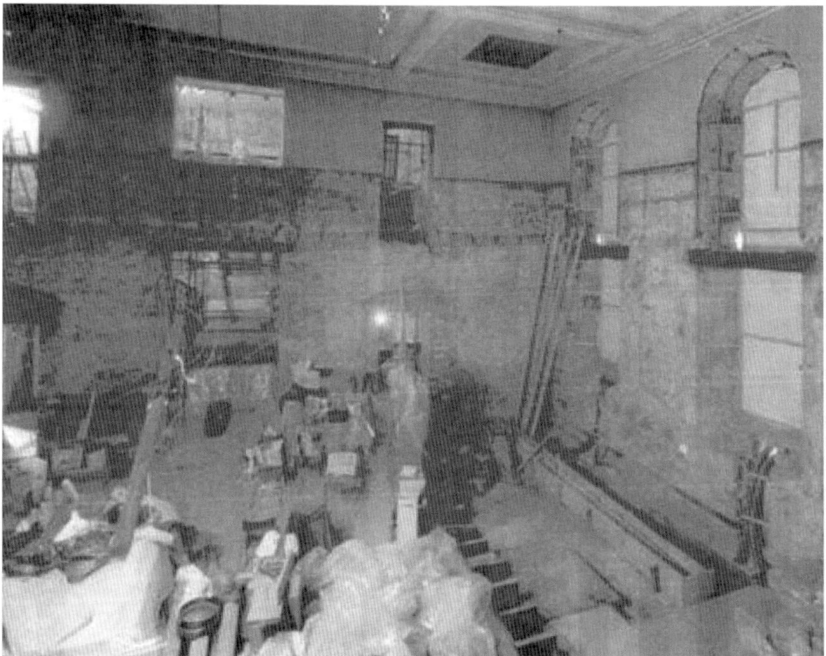

# Chapter One

## Early Recollections

The summers were long and hot, so warm one could possibly fry an egg on the pavement, and no one dare go without sandshoes or else tender young feet would blister on the country bitumen roads. School holidays lasted eight weeks in those far-off, bygone days, and we made the most of them, fishing for trout in the burn at the bottom of the garden, climbing the trees in the copse across the fields, or help pick pea pods, brambles and apples for jelly. In the long evenings, the dog was taken out for walks over the fields, and then it was back to play on the swing in the yard before being called inside for the night.

Being so high up in the hills, the winters were very cold, and we were the first in the Central belt of Scotland to see the snow. Sometimes, the snow was so hard packed that a pathway had to be shovelled out to the gate. Walls of snow were three feet plus on either side in height. To a young child's mind, it was exhilarating. It was always great fun building 'igloos' with blocks of glistening white granite, as we were wrapped up from head to toe with hats, gloves and scarves and little black lacing boots.

Friday at 4 o'clock, after school, saw us walk up the long hill to the local farm for a large can of buttermilk. Friday evening was baking night, when the smell of soda scones, treacle scones, and pancakes, wafted through the house. These were all baked on a griddle heated by a primus stove – no quick gas cookers in the country. It was open fired ranges or any alternative one had to hand.

We, as a family, had moved from Uplawmoor in Renfrewshire to Slamannan, Stirlingshire 'up the braes' as it is commonly known in that part of the world. My father always wanted to 'better' himself, and moved on as a lucrative new post presented itself. Daddy had landed the job of being head gardener of a large estate in the country, and we lived in the lodge house, which had upstairs and a very large 'secret cupboard'. To my childlike mind, everything in my garden was rosy. However, this second move was to cause some life-changing events.

Life was happy and good. One day, a 'Mission' came to the village. Every home was visited, and an invitation given to come along and hear the gospel. Before this time, my mother had attended some Salvation Army meetings with her sister in Greenock and loved the singing, etc. so she had an idea what the 'mission' entailed. My father knew little about the gospel having grown up in a large fishing family in Aberdeen, and as a young man had moved to the west coast on completion of his apprenticeship to work in gardening.

He loved the 'Kirk' (a Scottish church) in the village and was soon an elder in the local Church of Scotland, plus the Session Clerk. On a Sunday morning, my mother, father, brother and I sat in the fourth front wooden pew, listening to Rev Cameron's sermon. The church would be filled with people from all walks of life from gentry to the local tramp. The building was small and everybody knew everyone else. Only on special occasions, the gallery would be filled and that mostly by onlookers when a wedding was taking place.

*While the earth remains, seedtime and harvest, cold and heat, winter and summer, and day and night shall not cease (Genesis 8:22).*

I just loved the Autumn Harvest service. To see the front of the church packed with sheaves of corn and wheat, all different kinds of vegetables and fruits piled up row upon row. I can still smell the freshness and see the vibrant colours and contrasts. Pride of place was given to the very large marrows, leeks, courgettes, kale and curly greens. Also, carrots, beetroot, turnip and swedes, potatoes by the hessian sack load of different varieties. To a child's eye, it was like a theatre full of actors ready to perform a play! Perfume from the flowers wafted across the chancel, as we entered the church and into the buzz of admiration and excitement.

After the Harvest Thanksgiving Service, I had the pleasure as a small child of going with my father to deliver some of the goodies to the congregation the following week. People of the area were so thankful to receive – some never went to church and others could not attend because of ill health, but were greatly appreciative of the gifts. It was the only time I was allowed to use my mother's lovely egg basket to help carry the fruit, vegetables and flowers.

At Church, attendance cards were marked with a cross when we entered the vestibule. Also, another card was marked with a gold star if we went to the Sunday School after the morning service in the hall across the road. It had been a long time since breakfast, and we would run home after 2 p.m., very hungry and looking forward to home made soup. Lunch was special on Sundays as, in the winter, there was usually a steamed pudding with custard, or jelly with fruit in the warmer weather. In the afternoon, unless it was raining hard, it was the done thing to take a brisk walk along the country roads stopping to chat to passing villagers. Everything was quiet and leisurely, but it was not to remain that way for long.

*Your word is a lamp to my feet and a light to my path (Psalm 119:105)*

One night, I woke up abruptly with loud voices coming from the living room. My mother had gone to the mission with a friend and 'got saved'. My father in no way approved of this 'getting saved' business, and all hell let loose in our otherwise peaceful home that night. As a young child, I did not understand what was going on, all I knew was that fear came into my little heart at that time, and our otherwise normal household was turned upside down. Things did not get any better.

My mother continued going to the mission and wanted my father to go with her, but he was having none of it. "What would the church folk think? and he was part of the 'Mason's group', and 'that other group' believed in water baptism, but his church believed in christening! It was just too much to take in, this new phenomenon! My father often tended the minister's garden on an evening, and went into the manse for tea afterwards. No doubt, they had extended theological discussions regarding this 'new religion'.

There was no other church in the village except the two 'big churches' and the Roman Catholic Chapel. This was a new nonpareil! Revivals had broken out in Sunderland in Rev Boddy's church, and in the Hebrides with Duncan Campbell in Scotland, books had been written about Smith Wigglesworth's ministry of healing, Kathryn Kuhlman in America had been mightily used and had a ministry of leading people into the Gifts of the Holy Spirit and healing. Earlier Carrie Judd Montgomery set up Houses of Healing such as Beulah Heights. Oral Roberts (who is still alive today) had a great healing ministry, and set up a Prayer Tower in Tulsa, Oklahoma and people were being converted through seeing the many miracles. The winds of change were blowing towards Britain.

*For we cannot but speak the things which we have seen and heard (Acts 4:20)*

One night, my mother came home having received a vision of the Risen Christ, and He beckoned her to come to Him and embrace all that He had to give her. She arrived home having been 'baptised in the Holy Spirit' and speaking in other tongues the beautiful language of heaven. The more radiant and anointed she got, the angrier my father became. This was too much for him, and life from then on took a downward spiral. He could not understand why my mother had to attend this new 'Apostolic Church' that had opened up in the village. We three continued going to the Church of Scotland on a Sunday morning, and my mother to the new Pentecostal church, which incidentally, was held in Harry the barber's old shop, as he had retired. She took me as a young child to the new church, because she felt that I should accompany her in the evening.

Even as a young girl, I loved the Saviour and wanted to follow Him all the days of my life. My father always encouraged us to read, and often bought me educational books, which I devoured and read over and over again. One special book, which I still have, and which takes pride of place on the bookshelf in the study, is 'Through the Bible' by Theodora Wilson. I remember going on the bus to Falkirk one Saturday morning near Christmas time with my Daddy, and he took me into this Aladdin's cave (Dunn & Wilson) of books, geographical, historical, autobiographical, and fictional, pens, pencils and notepads, jotters, bibles, calendars etc. To my young eyes, it was a veritable paradise!

All during those formative years, my mother made friends with the people from the new church, and I with a girl called Margaret. We went to school together, played together, went to church together and talked plenty about what we wanted to be when we 'grew up'. On cold, wet, wintry afternoons, we would line up our teddies and dolls, play the pedal organ, sing a sacred song from the Redemption hymn book, take turns at speaking the sermon, and have 'church' in the front room. We even took up the collection (buttons), and by our way of it, send it to missionaries in darkest Africa, it was good stuff!

As it happened, we both married a 'MacDonald' and 'Macdonald' respectively. Our mothers were known as Mrs Milne and Mrs Adamson, as it was thought proper to call ladies by their married name.

In those bygone days, you were expected to go to the 'Open Air meeting' before church in the evening. I vividly remember, on more than one occasion, standing in front of the tall village clock, at the cross where four roads meet, as a young girl holding my mother's hand while eggs and rotten tomatoes were thrown at us because of the witness for Jesus Christ!

On the following Monday morning at school, I was bullied mercilessly as word went round a village like wildfire, and my face was often the colour of a tomato with all the ribbing! But the elders and saints still carried on in triumph and victory, knowing that the enemy of our souls did not like the witness, as it was having a great affect on the lives of men and women. People were converted, lives and families were marvellously changed, and the little church grew.

Because the Free Church and the Church of Scotland were amalgamating, a manse became available for rent, and so it was decided by the authorities that we as a family could move into the now empty manse. What fun we had sliding down the bannister when no one was looking. There were trees to climb, outhouses to explore, and uniquely, a black coloured telephone sat in the hall. Christmas time in the very large front room with a coal fire burning and a decorated tree together with hot juice and homemade scones and jam seemed to be the answer to everything on a very cold, snowy December day. Life seemed good again.

*Will a man rob God? (Malachi 3:8)*

About this time, my father found out a most outrageous thing. My mother was 'tithing' her housekeeping money to the new church! He had never heard of such goings-on in his whole life! He, like all 'good Christians', put two shillings into the church envelope and that was considered to be generous! What wars and rumours of war went on behind closed doors one shall never know. This new revelation about believing the whole Word of

God was too much for my father, and he struck out at my mother in sheer disbelief. Embracing the full-orbed truth of the Word is costly. Today, people do not realise the price some had to pay in order to keep the Pentecostal vision alive. It is taken for granted, some even adopt the attitude *"I can take it or leave it". Not so in God's book. He says, "Exhort them to continue in the faith, and that we must* ***through much tribulation*** *enter into the kingdom of God" (Acts 14:22).*

It was agreed that my mother and I should go to Aunt Maggie's in Port Glasgow for two or three weeks leaving my father and brother at home. I remember the morning well. It was a Monday (after an especially blessed Sunday), and the headmaster came to the classroom door and asked me to collect my school bag and coat, as my mother was waiting for me at the school gates, and that I would be away for a few weeks. What could have happened to cause this expulsion?

At 8.30 a.m., when I left the house that morning, everything seemed fine, and then my world literally caved in. I loved my school; I came in early to give out the books and then waited behind class every day to clean Miss Young's blackboard. We prefects did this as an extra because we loved and respected our teachers. To leave my friends and my school seemed too high a price to pay – it was unbearable!

When Mum and I left on the bus to travel to Renfrewshire, Daddy was working and I never got a chance to say "cheerio" to him. I wept bitter tears and even reviled the Christ who saved me.

The Daddy, whom I loved very much and admired greatly, was to be left behind to look after himself, and I did not know when I would see him again. In all of this, there was no word of separation or anything untoward as deep down my parents loved each other and were happy together, apart from 'this new religion'.

No one knows the half of the persecution that transpired at that time for embracing and declaring the whole Word of God. Yes, there were the revivals, but some had to pay a high price for what we take for granted today. God forbid that we would ever take the moving of the Spirit of God lightly. How the Holy Ghost of God must be grieved when even some of His own blood-bought children turn their backs on His precious Gifts and despise the anointing of the Lord, and the enduement of power from on high. It was not all singing, going to the exciting new Conventions, reading about the latest miracles. As found in Ephesians chapter four, verses eleven and twelve – Apostles were opening new churches, Prophets prophesying the mind and will of the Holy Spirit, Evangelists holding Rallies, Pastors caring for the new converts and the Teachers of the Word expounding the scriptures. This new emerging church had the dynamics of the 33 A.D. fellowship!

Right away, I was enrolled in a local school in Greenock so as not to lose any education, and my mother soon settled in to her new routine. In those days, there was great talk about the soon-coming of the Lord, and it seemed so to be as we, my three cousins and I, listened behind the closed sitting room door when we should have been in bed, to Auntie Maggie and Mum talking about how the Lord was calling people to Himself in a new way and beseeching them to follow Him to lands across the sea as missionaries for the Gospel sake. My mother appeared to be so holy to my three cousins that they called her 'the Holy Ghost', and whenever she was present, they tried never to tell lies or do bad things. We were all only young, but the fear of the Lord was present to chasten and correct us.

A few weeks had passed when, one Saturday morning, I heard a great commotion at the kitchen window. My Daddy was walking along the avenue towards the house with big parcels. When I saw him, my heart nearly burst with excitement. This was my Daddy come for Mum and me to take us home!

It was decided that things could be worked out with respect and tolerance. I was not altogether sad at leaving the town, as I loved the countryside and I had missed my friends. School is a great leveller, and once more, I had to make up for all the time I had been away. Someone else had the job of prefect, so I no longer was the teacher's pet, but I had learned invaluable lessons that neither money nor education could buy.

The dreaded Qualifying Examinations were looming ahead, and to get a good grade was very important as it meant going to a High School or the local Technical School and I knew where I wanted to go. So it was head down in earnest. Also, the village 'Crowning of the Queen' ceremony took place at the local Gala Day in the public park in June after the exams, at which there were races, games, stalls and food for all. Depending on the mark received, the pupils with the highest grades were picked for the Queen and her attendants. The real race was on as this was rivalry in earnest!

At Assembly one Friday morning, the names of those who would be in the 'Queen's Procession' were read out. Consternation and unbelief engulfed me when my name was read out to be attendant to the Queen, just before school broke up for the holidays. It was if the Lord honoured and gave me His blessing and made up to me for all the unhappiness and tears of the past months. I had to learn quickly "*in whatsoever state ... to be content*".

My parents took me to Falkirk and bought an outfit befitting a lady-in-waiting to the Gala Queen. I remember coming home and going into my bedroom, falling on my knees and thanking God for His preserving hand and goodness to me as a young girl, and prayed for the salvation of my father and brother. On the big day, we drove down the village streets in a gold carriage drawn by two shire horses. As young girls, we thought we were the bees' knees as we waved and smiled to the crowds who had lined the country roads. All was well with the world once more.

## Big decisions

- *The steps of a good man are ordered by the Lord and he delights in His way (Psalm 37:23).*

The time was near when my brother and I would be making decisions about our future careers. Ever mindful of this, my father applied for a post in Stirlingshire where there were good schools and Colleges in the area, and was successful in obtaining a much sought-after position. I remember well the day Mum and I went with him to Viewforth offices in Stirling, as he was to be interviewed for the third time, because his name was on the selective 'short-list'. What joy when he came out beaming with the news that he had been successful in obtaining the post. Now we could move and settle in the Larbert area. I also remember the love and joy coming back into our home at this news.

Elizabeth Coatsworth penned a beautiful saying, which is appropriate here:

> I saw the lovely arch of rainbow span the sky.
> The gold sun burning as the rain swept by.

The day came when we 'flitted', and crammed all our furniture into a little two-bedroomed cottage, which my father had been informed 'was only a temporary measure until the house promised was built'. A couple of years later, we finally moved into our newly built home. I have fond memories of those times during the summer when we picked apples, fruit from the blackcurrant bushes, redcurrants, strawberries, raspberries, gooseberries, rhubarb, marrows from the cloches to be stuffed for dinner, tomatoes from the greenhouse, red, yellow and even white.

I remember about this time, the English teacher in my new High School asking us to write an essay about who we would want to be and why. I wrote that I did not really want to be anyone else. I was very happy with the life I was living. I felt fulfilled and content. I had peace in my heart and the knowledge of sins forgiven, also the Holy Spirit's leading and guiding. Her comments regarding my essay were of a surprised and guarded nature!

My father was in his new job, my mother in her new Pentecostal church, (which was becoming more acceptable by this time), my brother in college and yours truly in the High School. All was well. Although my father never fully came to terms with the 'tongues business', he never kept my Mum back from following the Lord in the way that she wanted. He still attended the Church of Scotland, now as an elder in Mr McPhail's church, who lived next door to us. At times, my Dad even came to the occasional Convention, but usually had a few comments afterwards, some of which were not altogether wholesome, but that was all right.

At about this time in a Convention in Perth, when I was in my early teens, I was baptised in the Holy Spirit, and I knew that I had entered a new dimension in my Christian life that enabled me to experience a strength I had not known before. This revolutionised my prayer life and brought me closer to the Lord Jesus Christ. However, something was to happen in my father's life that would change him dramatically – and our home forever.

In those days, in the 1950's, parents never really talked about money or personal things in front of the children, so sometimes, we were kept in the dark as to what was really going on. One morning, there was a commotion outside and the fire brigade was called to that part of the estate garden where the greenhouses and potting shed were located. There had been a fire, and everything had literally gone up in smoke.

My father came back to the house very drawn and upset. Many people did not believe in banks in those days and kept money under the mattress, in shoe boxes or somewhere they thought would be safe. My father kept his hard-earned money in an old jacket in the potting shed beside the greenhouses, which housed the open-fired boiler. All his precious savings had gone up in smoke!

Daddy had occasionally worked extra hours or sometimes, was a judge at local flower shows, and his financial reward would be added to the pile! Because we lived in a tied house (that is, one which went with the job), he had his mind set on buying a cottage when he retired – hence the cache of savings. As well as being thrifty, he was also generous, and always had a bag of sweeties in his pocket to give away. His favourite sweets were mixed caramels and Turkish delight.

## *With God, all things are possible*

Two or three years later, Americans came to live in Fairlie House, next to where my father worked in Torwood Hall. One winter, as they were going back to the USA for a holiday, they asked my father to look after the house and check the grounds while they were away. It was almost time for their return, when the police called at our house to inform my father that there had been a burglary and that the best silverware, paintings, jewellery, and other valuable items had been stolen. I was never told about the burglary, I only heard the whispers in the front room and all conversation stopped as my friends and I came in from school.

As there were no other fingerprints except my father's found on the premises, and no forced entry gained, my father was speculatively accused of the burglary, and a date was made for him to go to Court in Stirling. This took its toll on his health at this time, as he was by nature a sensitive and proud man, and also held in high esteem in the village.

One day, not knowing anything of this, I came home from school to see, through the crack of the front room door, the pastor of the Apostolic church, and my mother and father on their knees praying! What in all the earth could have happened to bring my father to his knees? God's ways are past finding out, and if you do not come the easy way, sometimes He takes you the long hard road. That afternoon, my Dad gave his heart to the Lord. Man's extremity is God's opportunity. They were praying that God would expose the thieves, and that my father would be vindicated before the case came to Court. A tall order, but God does hear and answer prayer. With God, nothing is impossible!

A few weeks later, there was a road traffic accident in the south of England, and when the police examined the cars involved, there, in the boot of one of the cars, was some of the silverware, expensive paintings and jewellery! Word finally filtered through to the office concerned that the Court case be thrown out and Mr Milne be totally exonerated. The church rejoiced at the wonderful answer to prayer. We sometimes forget that God sees and knows all, and that He can and will intervene on our behalf when we turn to Him.

The book of Job, the 23rd chapter and verse 10 says, "*But He knows the way that I take, when He has tested me, I shall come forth as gold*".

The trials and experiences that we went through at that time, taught us to cling to the Rock of Ages and never let go until we saw God's hand at work in our lives for good. When we trust Him implicitly, and we have nowhere else to turn and no one else to turn to, His word is sure which says, "*I will never leave you nor forsake you*".

During this time, my brother had been 'called up' for Army Service and was seconded to the Argyle and Sutherland Highlanders in Stirling Castle initially, for training, and then posted abroad to British Guyana, South America after a few months. Like all mothers, my mother missed him being around the house, whistling the latest songs, cleaning his racing cycle, bringing his friends into the back yard with their bicycles, and generally helping out around the house.

*Death intervenes*

Time came for me to leave High School and go to College. I enrolled in McLay's College in Falkirk to do an accredited accelerated Commercial Course, which I enjoyed very much. After graduation, I joined the ranks of people who were paid for what they had been trained to do. It seemed to me the world was my oyster, and I was enjoying life.

By this time, I had left the Pentecostal church, joined the local Baptist Church and, following Jesus' example, was baptised in water. Being a teenager, I guess I wanted, as I thought, the best of both worlds, and God allowed me to taste and see. Outwardly, I appeared happy, but inwardly I had lost the sweet comfort of the Holy Spirit in my life, and I missed His Presence so much, but at that time, I would not have admitted it to anyone.

One Sunday morning during the morning service in the local Baptist Church, I was approached and asked to go home as there was some news waiting me. A friend accompanied me to the gate, only to discover that my father, who had been in hospital, had died that morning in Falkirk Royal Infirmary. I was devastated! I loved my father dearly, and I was the apple of his eye. He was the one who had encouraged me to read good books, and to learn to read music and to play the piano and the violin. The worry of the last few years had taken its toll, and he had developed an ulcer with complications. My mother and an elder from the church were with him when he went to be with the Lord. He was only 47 years of age, my mother 45 years, and I a teenager. I broke my heart, and it took me years to get over the grief of losing my precious daddy. Who would listen to my questions now, or encourage me to practise my music, give me advice, or chat to me about the latest bit of village news? No one takes the place of a good father. Something died in me that day. But God has a way of turning things round for good.

*Blessed is the man whose strength is in You ... as they pass through the valley of Baca (Psalm 84:5-6)*

Life for my mother and I changed from that time. My brother Alex had married Jean, and was making a new life for himself, setting up house in the village. As we lived in a tied house, my mother and I were given a few months grace to find another place to live. Mum also went into hospital about this time to have an operation, and I went to stay with a friend of the family until she got better, which was about a year later. Because of the grief and illness, Mum could not work and widows did not receive much by way of financial help at that time to keep us. During this period, I was employed by the Health Board and the wages were not very grand, so I kept looking for a post with a better salary.

One day, whilst reading the local Falkirk Herald newspaper, I saw a job advertised for a secretary to the manager of the new Colgate-Palmolive Company, which had just come to town, and the wages were double my present salary. I applied and got an interview, which I felt went quite well. A few days later, I received word that I was unsuccessful. Had I not trusted God to help my Mum and me at this time? Oh yes, I had prayed and bombarded heaven, but seemingly to none effect. I comforted myself with the fact that over 200 applicants had also applied for the post, but at least I had reached the short list. I ran to the throne of grace and poured out my heart to the Lord, and in my innocence asked "why?"

Six months passed, when out of the blue, I received a letter asking me to come for another interview, as the girl who had been given the post of personal assistant to the manager the first time round was emigrating to America!

The job was mine, and I started three weeks later. Not only did I have an excellent salary, but also on Fridays, I could order any product that Colgate-Palmolive produced at half price! I proved this verse to be true: "*The king's heart is in the hand of the Lord, as the rivers of water, He turns it wherever He wishes*" (Proverbs 21:1).

My Aunt Maggie, Uncle Jim, and my now four cousins who lived in Port Glasgow, had always been very close to us as a family. My favourite Aunt Maggie, who had helped Mum and me so many years before, developed cancer, and went to be with the Lord the very same week as my father. They were about the same age. We were all devastated at that awful news. Two funerals in the one week – Lord, life is almost unbearable! My mother losing her husband and sister within days. Our lives were being ripped apart. Somehow, we must pick up the pieces and begin living again.

## *Invitation to a Saturday night youth meeting*

I was invited by some friends to go with them to the Tent Hall in Glasgow, to a Saturday night meeting. Nothing unusual about that. We met up in the city, had a meal and then were off to this meeting place. When we arrived at 'the tent', there were hundreds of young people from all different churches and towns and villages. John Moore was the Superintendent, and everyone adored him. He led the meetings of approximately 1500 people of all age groups. We began to go there quite often on a Saturday evening and enjoyed every minute of it. By attending these meetings, it brought me back to my first love, and I expressed the desire to return to the little Pentecostal church. It was not long before I received a new anointing of the Holy Spirit's power to serve my Lord and witness for Him. He healed my broken heart piece by piece.

During the summer, I had gone to a camp fellowship with friends from Airdrie, and we agreed to meet up at Tent Hall and exchange some photographs, which we had taken that year in Scarborough. Before we went for the train or bus back home, a crowd of us usually met at R.S. McColl's tearoom or, the Brethren cafe, called Miss Buick's, for coffee, which enabled us to mix with other Christians, make new friends, and exchange photographs and news.

Tent Hall started at 7 p.m. sharp and finished at 9 o'clock, so we had a good hour before we ran for the train to Buchanan Street Railway Station. One Saturday evening, it was absolutely pouring with rain and we were spilling over on to Argyle Street, arm in arm, singing the latest choruses, when I heard a voice behind me say, "Can I get under your umbrella, blondie?" To my surprise, it was the young man whom I had espied earlier in the meeting, and Marina had informed me, "all the girls want to go out with him, but he is a bit elusive". My reply to that handsome young man was that I did not know him and there was no room for another! Not taking no for an answer, after tea and cake at R.S. McColl's tearoom in Union Street, he (Duncan) said he had been invited to a party and, as he didn't have a partner, would I accompany him next week? Not to be deterred, he gave me his telephone number to let him know by the Wednesday.

As it turned out, I went to the party, and our friendship grew from there on. Soon after this, I met his Mum and Dad and brother Robin, and got on very well with all of Duncan's family. Our relationship blossomed, and after two years, we were engaged in the middle of Hogganfield Loch, Glasgow, sitting in a rowing boat, with Duncan at the helm. Carefree and happy days indeed! My happiness had returned. Mum and Duncan enjoyed each other's company enormously, and spoke often round the Word. We usually visited Auntie Mary on a Saturday, as she lived quite close to the Cathedral in Ladywell Court. We also laughed a lot, as Duncan had a way of telling a story and making it hilariously funny.

Three years after we met, we were married in the Apostolic Church in North Frederick Street, Glasgow. Our reception was in the famous Ca'dora Hotel.

My friend Nadine was bridesmaid and Douglas was Duncan's

best man. The day was warm and sunny on that September day, and we were walking into a new life together in God.

We spent our honeymoon in Swansea, because we felt that it was God’s will for Duncan to attend Pen-y-groes Bible College. We knew that we had the call of God on our lives, so I remained at home and sent his fees monthly, whilst he studied. After our marriage, I received a substantial rise in salary, for which we were thankful. God always met and supplied our every need.

On arrival at Glasgow Central Station, Duncan’s Dad met me and took me home for tea and comfort. The journey back to Scotland had been a formidable one on my own, especially having left my new husband to bravely do what was in our hearts. But we knew the Lord was in everything – Duncan settled into his studies and I held the fort at this end. On reflection, even at the onset of our marriage, God was preparing us for a life of faith, but we did not recognise it at the time.

# Chapter Two

## The call to service

Knowing that there was a call on our lives, we prayed a lot and read the Word together, ever seeking God's will for our lives. Duncan went to Bible School in South Wales, and I continued working to support him in his studies. We moved to Irvine in Ayrshire when our little son Gillies was two years old. We had a new house and Duncan had a new job; we were now both in the Apostolic Church in Kilwinning and all was well. My mother loved to come to Irvine and stay with us for weeks at a time, and we loved having her. We would talk about the Word of God and 'end-times'. Auntie Mary, who was blind, was also a favourite visitor. Duncan's Mum and Dad would visit with Robin, and we would enjoy good conversations, good food and plenty of laughs.

Life at our new church was spiritually stimulating, and we quickly made friends. At New Year, we used to take the children (Elaine and Gillies) to Duncan's parents in Glasgow. They gladly looked after them while went to the great New Year Convention Meetings in the North Frederick Street church in the city (no longer there), heard the wonderful exposition of the Word of God and listened to the Word through the prophets. The singing was second to none, as one's spirit soared with the anointed hymns and choruses ably led by the Leader of Song, Pastor Andrew Turnbull, one of the early pioneers of the Movement.

This was always a precious time for us, and an inspiring occasion, as it crowned the New Year with God's Divine Presence and favour. We also had the blessing of staying with Auntie Mary (who lived near the Cathedral), and my mother would travel from Stirlingshire to be with her. We all meet up as a family at Nana's. New Year's Day was extra special, as Nana would cook an amazing dinner. More family would join us from Cardross and Balloch. We would sing round the piano and have shortbread and ginger wine. Happy times with plenty of banter and laughter.

At times during the Convention, the Lord spoke through the prophet and called certain people into office in the church. On one of those occasions, nine young men were called into service in the local assemblies. However, Duncan was not one of them, and he was so disappointed! He was indeed pleased for those whom the Lord had blessed, but wondered in his heart why God had not spoken to him. As he went downstairs to the cloakroom to get his coat, he felt a hand on his shoulder, and to his amazement, it was the President of the church, Pastor Tom Saunders. He said, "Duncan, do not be disappointed that the Lord did not speak to you tonight. You are a marked young man, and He will make His will known to you in due season". He was greatly encouraged by that timely remark.

A few months later, after seeking the will of God for our lives, Duncan said to me one morning, "Greta, I've had a strange dream. I saw the overseer of the Ayr Assembly rise up from behind the communion table, walk to the back of the church, lift his coat and hat, put them on and, without looking back, walk out of the door. Then I saw myself walk to the front of the church, and take his place between the elders". We knew this could only mean one thing, but hid all these things in our heart without telling anyone, trusting God all the way.

Three months later, the doorbell rang at 10 o'clock one night. The Pastor of the district stood there and asked if he could come in. There had been a meeting that day in the Glasgow church, and the prophet of the Lord had spoken during the meeting. He said that He would have his servant Duncan MacDonald be anointed as overseer of the Ayr Assembly, and the present overseer be removed back to the Kilmarnock church. Duncan therefore was never called into the eldership as the others were, but appointed straight into the oversight with elders, evangelists, deacons and deaconesses under his care. What a day of celebration when he was set apart, hands laid on for ministry and anointed with oil. The Lord had been glorified in the midst of His people with the dream from heaven come to fruition.

Duncan and I always believed that the House of the Lord should be as good, if not better than our own homes. So, a few years into the ministry of overseer, it was decided locally to give the church building a good face-lift. Panel the walls, paint the rest, carpet the floors and put on new doors. At the beginning, everyone was enthusiastic, but gradually the people tailed off, leaving Duncan and one other person to continue the work. Eventually, it was very good, lovely and clean and modern.

*Illness strikes*

September 9th was our Wedding Anniversary, and Duncan decided to finish off the work, which he had been doing in the church. So, after working all day and hastily downing a quick meal, he drove to the Ayr church in order to try and wind everything up, and then drove back home to Irvine. It was quite late by the time he arrived home, and I saw immediately that he was extremely tired. He said he was just going to go to bed, and did not even want a drink of milk or tea.

Five minutes later, I also retired for the night. When I went into the bedroom, I saw Duncan slumped over the bed. I recognised some other symptoms, so I shouted on the Name of Jesus, pleaded the blood of Christ and commanded his spirit to come back into his body. He rallied round, and I immediately telephoned for an ambulance to take him to hospital to have everything checked out. He was there for three weeks, and eventually discharged.

Following his discharge, he was nursed back to some sort of normalcy, although he said he did not feel completely well, and that he tired very easily. It turned out that he had suffered a severe sub-cranial haemorrhage. We prayed that God in His mercy would heal him because there was no way he could ever work again feeling the way he did. Around that time, we heard about a move of God in England, so Nana offered to look after the children while we travelled south by train.

Friends from Altrincham had told us that there was someone coming to Manchester to hold special healing meetings; Trevor Dearing was his name, and would we like to go? When we arrived, we discovered that all the tickets had been taken and that there were no seats left. Not to be deterred, someone else came with the news that an Anglican vicar – Colin Urquhart – was also holding healing meetings in Manchester University on Sunday afternoon, and if we were willing to queue, we could possibly get in.

On arrival, we sat near the back of the lecture hall, and were immediately blessed by four nuns behind us singing, "His name is higher than any other, His name is Jesus, His name is Lord". That set the stage for us. Colin came out in his robes and spoke on 'Faith of the God kind', after which, he invited all those who desired healing to come out initially for an anointing of faith. Duncan did not want to go out, so I went on his behalf, and was really blessed in my spirit. Then Colin called for those who had a need to come to the front for the laying on of hands, and we both went out together. As the servant of God approached Duncan, I extended my faith towards him, because I knew how much he needed a mighty touch from God. Colin just laid his hands on him as he prayed, and commanded the infirmity to go in Jesus' name. Duncan went down like a feather, so gentle and peaceful. He later told the story how, as he lay quietly praising God for all His goodness, the tight band that he felt constantly around his head just snapped, and he was free from the fears that had ruled his life every day for months. Hallelujah, what a Saviour!

The morning after we arrived back home, Duncan met one of our neighbours, Mrs Ness, and she noticed that he looked really well. She asked what had happened to him, since she used to see him walking around Ravenscroft either with the aid of a walking stick or taking my arm for support. Over a cup of coffee, Duncan told her all about what the Lord had done, much to the delight of Mrs Ness.

At that time, Duncan worked for Hyster Ltd. in Irvine, and, if the truth were known, they did not expect to see him back at work. The next day, he went to see Mr Cameron, the Director, who was so surprised to see Duncan up and about that he said, "Come into the Board Room, we are just about to have a meeting, and you can tell us what happened"! What a platform for a great story, giving all the glory to God. It was agreed that Duncan should be given another job, and that he could begin the following week. God is still in the healing business!

### *Death in the family*

The biggest trial of our lives was still to face us. Nine months later, on a Sunday afternoon in May 1978, our little son Duncan Max was killed, and went to be with the Lord. As can be imagined, our whole family was in total shock. We could not believe what had happened – our son and the children's little brother had actually gone. Duncan, in his wisdom, took me to see Duncan Max two days later. Before we went into the parlour to view, he prayed that Max's little smile would return so that I would know it was undoubtedly our little darling boy, and be comforted. The little crooked laughter lines were there, and I was at peace. The little chubby hands that used to hang round my neck were exactly his; so were the little fingers that strummed the red plastic guitar, which his Auntie Cassie had given him as he sang his favourite chorus, "We are complete in Him". He was truly safe in the arms of Jesus and in heaven with our loved ones who had gone on before. It was devastating for our children, and for a long time, one or two members of the family could not even talk about it, so deep was the pain. But God in His mercy, and with the passing of time, heals the broken hearted.

Duncan often received dreams and visions from the Lord, and here, I shall record one of the visions, which we believe the Saviour gave us to help us over the grief, and it may help any reader who has gone through a similar experience. Three days after the sad event, Duncan went upstairs after breakfast to pray, and while in prayer, he saw a beautiful grassy plain and clear blue sky unfold before him. He saw hundreds of children walking along, each one having an adult hand leading the way. Then out of the corner of his eye, he saw our little Duncan Max run to catch up with them. Suddenly, someone reached down, and lifted him up into his arms. Duncan clearly heard the words, "Who are you?" coming from little Duncan Max's lips, inquisitive as ever. The reply came back, "I'm Abraham", and he put him down. They then walked hand-in-hand together until out of sight.

When Duncan came downstairs, he told me what the Lord had shown him, but we both wondered why Abraham had come for our little treasure. We were soon to find out.

Once again, we travelled to Manchester with our older son and daughter. This time, we went by car, as Duncan senior was well by now. One evening, we went to a meeting at which a healing evangelist was ministering. Before he got up to minister, a local choir assembled on the stage and, with ages ranging from three to sixteen years, their opening piece was "I'm a son of Abraham". Now we understood that Abraham is privileged to welcome the children into heaven, because he was willing to sacrifice Isaac on the altar in obedience to God's command. We wept at God's dealings with us, and how awesome His ways. Yet again, another healing had begun.

The day before the tragedy happened, a friend and I had travelled to Glasgow on the Saturday to attend a women's rally. We decided to go early, have lunch and visit the Christian bookshop. It was while we were in the bookshop that my friend Margaret said to me, "You bought me something the last time we were here, now it is my turn, would you like one of those large posters?" On glancing through the pile, I decided on one depicting a large bunch of purple grapes attached to a leafy branch with the text – I am the vine and you are the fruit of the vine. When I came home, I put it up on the mantelpiece. Duncan said that he would make a frame for it, as he also liked it.

We decided to go back to the ministry meeting the following evening. Everyone was invited to write their prayer request on a card, and hand it over before the evangelist, Melvin Banks, prayed for the person. When it came to our turn to be prayed for, he asked the whole congregation to come to a hush, as this was a special request for inner healing for our two children and ourselves on the death of a son and brother. When the servants of God had finished praying for Duncan, he turned to thank them for the lovely gentle touch on his shoulder, and the peace that pervaded his entire being. The evangelist replied, "I did not touch you, because I saw that the Lord had sent His angel to minister to you, and he was the one who was comforting you".

When the Pastor's mother prayed for me, she said, "I see a picture of a large bunch of grapes, and the Lord is telling me that before fine wine can be poured out, the grapes have to be crushed, and out of this crushing experience, you will be as fine wine to the thirsty souls of men and women". What more can I say except that God is the only all-wise, all-knowing Creator. 'The Lord gives, and the Lord takes, blessed be the Name of the Lord'.

Only God knows, and we will never know, the thoughts that went through our two older children's young minds during that deep dark experience, their personal valley of Baca.

*Investiture*

Ten months later, Duncan and I were sitting quietly in the living room reading, after the children had gone to bed, when the telephone rang. I took the message. It was Nana (Duncan's mother) to say that they had some news for us, and it was good news. A letter had come from the Lord Chamberlain's office in Downing Street, London, to say that Duncan's father had been awarded the MBE, and would he reply in the affirmative. The Investiture would be held at Buckingham Palace, London, on 13th March 1979, at 10 a.m. Shenner's (Duncan's father) first reaction was that his colleagues at school had pulled a fast one on him, and were having a bit of a joke. Every cloud has a silver lining so the saying goes.

He had been awarded this medal in recognition of his extracurricular work among some of the poorer children in the city, by way of taking them abroad on holiday, while Nana went as nurse and counsellor to the children. Hundreds of his pupils had been taught the bagpipes and his dream was to see a Piping College. Today, there is an excellent facility in the city training all age groups. He also helped to raise money for the school pipe band's uniform of kilts, jackets and hats, as well as for instruments. We were so pleased for him because he had a big heart for people who needed that initial helping hand.

The next Saturday, we drove up to Glasgow early to see the letter for ourselves, and congratulate him on this great honour. It was family discussion time on what to do next and how to go about arranging travel etc.

It came to mind that my friend Nadine lived in London, and that perhaps she could tell us of a hotel where we could stay while we were there. Apart from husband and wife being allowed into the Palace, a further two members of the family were also allowed to be present. Shenner being the man he was, wanted us all to go, no one to be left out. So it meant eight of us going down to the metropolis by train together. Robin was courting Sandra at this time and so she was also included in the family group.

Where to stay was the big question, as we did not know the

hotels in London at all, or even if there was a special one near the palace into which we could book. I pondered over this problem for a while, and finally thought that the best thing to do was to telephone Nadine. She and her husband Martin were both in the police force, and I was certain that they were the best people to give us good advice.

How our God delights to surprise His children! When I contacted Nadine, she told me that Martin was now Chief of Police at the palace, and to come down a day or so earlier and he would take Shenner around the investiture area to put his mind at rest, as he was naturally a bit nervous. The icing on the cake was that we could all stay with Nadine and her family as they had plenty of room! Our God is a miracle working God. Nana and Shenner opted to stay at a nearby hotel as Shenner snored like a train coming round the corner at 120 miles per hour. Nana was very deaf when she took out her hearing aid, so it did not matter one way or another! They were happy and we were all delighted.

What a wonderful day Tuesday 13th March turned out to be. Olivia Newton-John and Michael Jackson were honoured also at that time. Shenner being a fan of Olivia managed to get a kiss on the cheek, and that really made his day. Duncan and Robin were also allowed into the Investiture, and they were so proud of their Dad. We four, Gillies, Elaine, Sandra and I happily stayed in the police office at the side of the palace until the celebrations were over.

The rain came pouring down towards the end, but we were happy that the smile of God's favour was upon us once more. We went to Mr Bumble's for a much-needed meal along with Nadine and Martin, taking photographs all the while for posterity's sake. Some important days can never be repeated, so, when you can enjoy the journey – enjoy the journey!

It was back to Kent to kick off the fancy shoes, have a bath, relax, and get packed up for the trek back home to bonnie

Scotland! It had been an experience of a lifetime, precious treasured memories. Looking back some twenty plus years later, it was wonderful having all the family together, sharing laughter. After our great sorrow, we felt some wounds had begun to heal and life was bearable again.

### *Moving house*

We wanted to move house and looked at property after property. Finally, there was one house that caught our attention in another village, and we liked it very much. We had put in a substantial offer, and felt fairly confident about it.

The solicitor had said that the house was ours, unless a cash buyer came by midday on the day of closure. To our absolute amazement, that very thing happened! We were stunned, as we had already measured for carpets and curtains etc., and could see ourselves in that particular house.

However, it was not to be our future home, so we just kept trusting and praying. Millions of people know the frustrations of buying (and selling a house), and we were no different.

Nevertheless, the right house soon came along quite unexpectedly, and on reflection, the four of us were absolutely delighted that we did not get the other house in Kilwinning, but waited for one in Irvine, which suited us much better. God picks the best for those who leave the choice to Him. We moved into our new home and soon settled down in Ravenscroft.

### *Changes in the ministry*

When seven years of ministry had been fulfilled in the Ayr assembly, we were invited to go to the Kilmarnock assembly in order to build up the church there. After a time of having no young people, the Lord sent in a goodly number, most of whom are serving the Lord today in their own sphere.

Towards the end of another seven years, we went through a particularly trying time. The Lord spoke (thank God for the gifts of the Holy Spirit) and said that out of this trying and difficult experience He would mould us and make us into the vessels of His choice, as He had a great plan for our lives. We were extremely encouraged by this word, and continued to keep Jesus Christ our Lord and Saviour uppermost in our experience.

The children were still young, and we took them with us wherever we went. We used to speak in the Sanquhar Assembly and encourage the saints there. Tommy and Mary Burns gave wonderful hospitality, no matter the weather. In the winter, the country roads were very bad, but in the car looking out, it was like a winter wonderland. As I write in 2007, most of the saints from that Assembly have gone to be with the Lord.

We remember Dumfries Assembly with great delight. Mr and Mrs Windsor lived outside the town and had a lovely house on the hillside. They were always kind to the children and we spent the afternoon between the meetings talking about Oral Roberts' ministry, Morris Cerullo's ministry and the latest healing evangelists. They were true saints of God, who loved the Lord with all their heart and soul, and feared His Name in the greatest sense of the word.

On various Sundays in the year, we would be sent to Clydebank, Cumbernauld, Greenock, or Uddingston to name but a few places to preach the Word. Duncan usually sang the latest hymns, while I played the organ or keyboard. We enjoyed life and met many precious people and our lives were enriched because of it. Similarly, speakers and their wives came to our local assembly, and we were always pleased to give hospitality and fellowship.

We were totally immersed in the work of the Lord. It was our life and we just loved the fellowship. We had many friends, and would go on holiday together and enjoy the blessings of the

Lord. We particularly enjoyed the Conventions. Perth Convention was particularly blessed, as was the Edinburgh Convention. Then there were the district conventions, women's rallies, evangelistic weekends, youth witness rallies, but the best of all for us was the New Year Convention in Glasgow, formerly held in North Frederick Street, and latterly Cathedral Street.

Two holidays stand out from the rest at that time. One was when we decided to go to Uncle Tom's Holiday Camp at Scarborough. There were the four of us, together with Mary and Jimmy Winning with their three children and Jimmy's mother. We departed in our second-hand cars on the long trek to Yorkshire around 10 o'clock at night, after only a few hours sleep. Three quarters of the way into the journey, the handbrake in our car refused to work, so it was foot pedal stuff all the way to Scarborough with its rolling hills and steep inclines! We sang songs about having the victory in all situations and circumstances until we finally arrived at Camp. Fortunately, there was a mechanic on site, and he quickly fixed the brake. The 'chalets', we discovered, were glorified garden huts with no amenities within 30 yards. Our children soon discovered the short cuts to all the running water areas!

The campers were from all walks of life; some of them had been going there for over twenty years. There were a number of pastors and evangelists, as well as people seeking the will of God for their lives, others just to chill out, and some like us, wanting the children to have a holiday and enjoy the break. The food was absolutely delicious and served in the lean-to conservatory dining area. Ministry was of the highest calibre, and there were separate meetings for the children. At the end of two weeks, we had forgotten all about the inconveniences we had encountered, because of the great blessings that we had received and the new friends we had made along the way. We arrived at the camp limping in more ways than one, but went home with new songs that we had learned through brother Kincaid.

Glasgow Fair fortnight meant you packed up and just went off into the sunset to enjoy your two weeks annual holiday. This time John and Betty Holden from Cumbernauld and Duncan and I planned to go to Bournemouth to a Christian Hotel. It was a very long drive, but on arrival, we discovered it was a lovely hotel and pleasantly situated. We spent a leisurely week with plenty of sunshine and laughs with photographs to prove it!

We thought that we would take a trip to the Isle of Wight seeing we were so near. What a beautiful island! Duncan and John were pleased to learn that cream teas were the order of the day, especially in the afternoon, just as we were arriving on the island.

As Betty and I waited to be served, Duncan saw a few nuns enjoying the afternoon delicacy, and, singing the latest charismatic chorus (His Name is higher than any other) he went towards them. To everybody's amazement, they wholeheartedly joined in, which resulted in a discussion about what the Holy Spirit was currently doing in the world at large. As we said afterwards, only Duncan could get away with a thing like that, as he had a way with people and carried a certain charisma to which strangers warmed and were not offended. Divine Appointment indeed!

On leaving Bournemouth, we headed back to North Yorkshire. We wanted to take Betty and John to Hollybush Camp for a few days, as they had never been before. On arrival, we found that everywhere was booked up; even all the caravans had been taken.Where to stay was the question in our minds, and so we had to look further afield. We had passed Sandhutton on the way, so we thought that we would backtrack and enquire whether there were any 'bed and breakfast' vacancies there. To our delight, there were two double rooms in the Old Coach House. Betty and John opted for the front room, and we had the cosy coomed-ceiling back room.

After breakfast on the last day of camp, Duncan and John went to pay the bill. Coming back out to the car to head off for home, Duncan said to me, "Greta, I feel impressed to go back into the kitchen and pray for the lady of the house". He retraced his steps, and went back into the house. As he emerged some time later, his face was wreathed in smiles. It had been so right to obey the Lord. The lady had been a widow for only a few weeks, and was feeling low, so Duncan asked her if he could pray for her, and she gladly agreed. After the short prayer and with tears in her eyes, she proceeded to tell him that the bedroom in which we had slept had been occupied by John Wesley on a few occasions as he went round the country preaching. His famous horse had been tethered in the now dilapidated stables at the back. It was all the more interesting to us as we both had dreams of the God-kind during the night. Duncan said afterwards that if he had not turned back, he would never have heard that remarkable story. The moral here being – listen for the whispers of Jesus.

Furthermore, one morning, Duncan said, "Greta, I had the most intriguing dream last night. I saw row upon row of jars of honey with their lids off and a spoon at the side of the jar. They were all marked differently – heather honey, Australian honey, mixed honey, etc. People came to sample this lovely manufactured honey. But the Lord drew my attention to a hive where the bees were busily buzzing in and out. They were very industrious, lively, with soft humming sound. The honey from the comb was clear, pure and sweet, not manufactured. The Holy Spirit spoke into my spirit and whispered, 'Why eat of the manufactured, when you can sup at the source?' What a revelation from the Divine!"

The interpretation means that not all 'religious groups' or 'Christian places' are of Him – seek out the best. Go to no uncommanded place. At all times, apply the principle of going for God's highest and best. Make sure that where you worship is a hive and not merely a 'honey pot'.

## *Dreams and Visions*

- *Joel 2:28-29 And it shall come to pass afterward that I will pour out My Spirit on all flesh; your sons and your daughters shall prophesy, your old men shall dream dreams, your young men shall see visions. And also on My menservants and on My maidservants I will pour out My Spirit in those days.*

"Your level of vision will determine whether God will work through you or around you", quotes Bill Wilson of Metro Ministries in The Bronx, New York.

It was New Year 1970. The old year had passed, with all its joys and challenges, and we were on the threshold of new possibilities and horizons. Six months had passed since the death of my mother, Agnes Milne, and she was sorely missed by all of us.

Before dawn broke, I had a dream-vision of a very large, square upper room. Through the gloom, I could barely make out the people sitting in the darkness. It appeared that they were totally dejected, bowed down with cares and fears, with nothing much left to live for.

Gradually, a great light flooded the room, and encircled the company of people. The weary became full of joy and hope, as a great swelling anthem of heavenly praise invaded their being. His awesome Majesty, King Jesus, by His mighty Holy Spirit, had come to dispel their darkness, and bring release to the troubled soul.

At last, they had met Someone who was greater than all their problems. They had met the One who died on the Cross of Calvary in their place, and had taken their sins, though many, away. The Deliverer had come in all His awesome fullness.

As I observed this amazing transformation, music and light fused together in effulgent glory. A great banner was emblazoned on the wall – *This is my desire for Irvine.* A verse of scripture pierced my being:

- For the vision is yet for an appointed time, but at the end it ill speak and will not lie, though it tarries, wait for it; because it will surely come. It will not tarry (Habakkuk 2:3).

When I related the above to a trusted friend, she agreed to wait on the Lord for a confirmation word. After a few days, my friend received the scripture from Ecclesiastes 11:1

- Cast your bread upon the waters for you will find it after many days.

At the time that this dream-vision was given, Duncan and I were actively engaged in an established apostolic church, and felt perfectly comfortable knowing that we were in the centre of God's will. We continued to serve the Lord in a leadership capacity for a further twelve years after the vision had been given, trusting all the while that what God had revealed, He was able to bring to pass, knowing His delays are not denials.

In August 1982, after attending a Convention in South Wales, we felt that God was directing our attention more and more to the people of the town in which we had lived for many years, and so we began to pray and wait on His leading. God impressed on us that it was His will to bring together people of all denominations and no denomination, under the Lordship of Christ, and encourage those who had no hope to trust in the living God as their Friend and Redeemer.

As we continued to wait before the Lord, we knew it would not be easy to uproot ourselves from the assembly of God's people in which we had faithfully worked for years. The fellowship to which we belonged was very precious to us, and we had many friends up and down the land as well as locally. We thought of the wonderful servants and handmaidens of God who had been an inspiration to us over the years and whom we highly respected. But God was calling us apart, to walk a lonely road, and at times, to be misunderstood. We realised that this was Decision Day, and that the fulfilment of the vision would entail a costly sacrifice.

The Investiture, Buckingham Palace, London

ISOM Graduation, June 2008

# Chapter Three

## Emmanuel Christian Centre

We invited the apostles and pastors of the Church to which we belonged to our home, in order to ask their blessing – which was given, but it was not thought appropriate at that time to have a 'Centre'. The Lord had already spoken into our heart that the Emmanuel Christian Centre would be more than a 'church'; it would be an end-time, apostolic, multi-purpose facility to accommodate the needs of the area. A 'church' is the people – a 'Centre' is the building! He desired to have a place opened up for 'the whosoever' seven days a week. Strictly speaking – it was God and us, sink or swim!

Shortly before we left the Fellowship, which we had attended since our teenage years, God spoke to us prophetically saying that He had seen the barrenness of the area, and He was giving us His rod, so that it might be used to liberate people from their bondage. If anyone asked who sent us, the reply was to be like Moses – The 'I Am that I Am' has sent us – and He would lead and guide!

God has a Divine Purpose for every believer. He wants everyone to experience the power that is available, and this was what we were about to see happen after twelve and a half years! Prayer and Bible Study began in our dinette with a small number of people who had a burden for the town.

While seeking the Lord in prayer on 21 February 1983, there was an assurance that we would have a place of meeting by 26 August 1983. God is precise about His dates. Further revelation came during the following months, showing that the work the Lord had for Ayrshire would be a Centre in Irvine where people could come, be encouraged, and go back to their churches strengthened. Some would stay and be part of a multi-faceted ministry Team.

The first confirmation of the fulfilment came when God laid it upon the hearts of two different people in England to supply the rent when God revealed where the new Centre was to be. After seeking God's face one day, Duncan heard the Spirit of God say that an effectual door would open, and that there would be roof lights the full length of the large room!

We spent days looking for the place that had been promised, at times weeping with the heaviness of the burden. Then, one Saturday morning in early August (1983), Duncan stopped to speak to a man in the High Street, and whilst they were talking, he happened to look across to the other side of the street at a specific building. He was strangely drawn to go and enquire regarding a room in the red sandstone building with a large bay window. The secretary of the then Conservative Rooms showed him the front lounge. This was large enough and available to rent. We were told that we would be notified in due course regarding the rental of the rooms if the trustees agreed.

In the meantime, we went to visit friends in England who had promised to pay the rent when we occupied the premises. They too shared the vision, knowing that it was of God, and they continued to pay the rent for the full seven years we were there.

We had searched the whole of the town until this particular Saturday morning. We just know that if you trust the 'I AM' implicitly, He makes no mistakes. When we went to view the rooms for the second time, the secretary said to us, "Oh, by the way, we have another, larger, room through those double doors". When the doors were opened, there, to our amazement, was indeed a very large, long room with roof lights all the way along the ceiling! We had lived in Irvine for years, parked our car opposite the property and never noticed the billiard room roof lights.

*152 High Street, Irvine*

On 22 August 1983, we were handed the keys to 152 High Street to commence the work that God had laid on our hearts.

The day had arrived when, instead of having Communion in the house, we had keys to rented property and could worship freely! There were ten of us who had a real burden for the town, and others who joined us from time to time. Small beginnings indeed

God's on-going purpose for the Emmanuel Christian Centre is to build a Team of Spirit-anointed, Spirit-led men and women who will be willing to be part of God's great end-time plan in these momentous days.

These are exciting times. Matthew 13:16-17 says:

- Blessed are your eyes for they see, and your ears for they hear. For I say to you that many prophets and righteous men have desired to see the things that you see and did not see, and to hear what you hear and did not hear.

At that time, we had Sunday Fellowship, Bible Studies plus a weekly Study for young men, prayer meetings, a ladies' night once a month (which went on to be the second 'Women Aglow' in Scotland). The highlight of the gatherings at that time was the 'Saturday at Seven' meetings. People came from far and wide to hear and see what God was doing. Guest speakers came to minister including Ken Stallard, author of 'The Road to Nowhere'; Professor Roy Peacock, who has the most amazing testimony of how God gave him a word of knowledge to solve a most difficult problem that had not been resolved for over four years by consultants in the aeronautics industry; and seminars led by Mike Costello from London, to mention only a few.

Christmas and New Year were wonderful times to be at 'the

Centre'. Banquets were laid on with the best of food, fun and fellowship. People came from North, South, East and West to hear of the great things God was doing in the midst of His people.

In the early days of the work, we both had secular jobs that we greatly enjoyed – but as the work progressed, we knew that God was calling us to lay down the secular work and trust Him in the area of finance. Five years into the work, the Lord spoke to me clearly and said that He wanted me to be available to Him twenty -four hours a day, seven days a week. I knew without a doubt what this would mean in terms of finance and personal dedication. The Lord also told me (because He knows our thoughts) that if I did not come the easy way, He would bring me the hard way!

Well, what do you think happened? I came the hard way and learned many valuable lessons along the journey of obedience. I finally said, "Lord, You win. Have my will, my all, take me as I am". That was in November 1987.

How faithful and merciful is our blessed Lord! I had developed a lump in my neck, and I needed an operation, because the tumour was sitting on the thyroid gland. One evening, as I was meditating on the ways of God, which are past finding out, the gentle whisper came that said, "I will heal you. A servant of mine, by the name of John Hutcheson, will come to the district, and he will have a word from Me for you. You will be healed at 10 p.m."! Had I really heard from God? By this time, the tumour had grown so big that I had to sleep sitting up with lots of pillows at my back to help my restricted breathing.

Two weeks before the operation was due, Duncan came in with a magazine. I happened to glance through it, and read that there as a meeting in Kilmarnock, and the guest speaker was listed as John Hutcheson! Because I was not one hundred percent sure whether it had been the Lord or my imagination that spoke to me,

I had not said anything to Duncan. But, on reading the advertisement, I was encouraged to tell him what God had whispered into my heart weeks previously. So, on the evening of the meeting, we collected two friends and made our way to the hotel.

During the time of sharing, John put down his notes and said, "Yesterday, when I was in prayer, the Lord impressed on me that there would be someone here tonight who had a lump on the neck and God was going to heal that person, would they come forward?" I got nudge-nudge, but I did not go forward because it was not nearly 10 o'clock, and anyway someone else could have the same symptoms as me. After some time, John said, "The person I referred to at the beginning has not come out yet, and so I will tell you another symptom that only you, God and I know about – this person is a lady".

I went forward! It was now 9.55 p.m. When he saw me standing in front of him, he said, "What are you doing here Greta? You look well". When I showed him the tumour, he said, "We will pray, and God will do the rest". I told him how the Lord had told me that he would come to Scotland and pray for me, and that I would be healed at ten o'clock! We prayed together in faith – it was ten o'clock precisely.

Two weeks later, I went to the local hospital as arranged, and after the initial examinations, I eventually had an operation on the thyroid gland. When the consultant subsequently came round the ward, he informed me that when they had opened me up, the tumour had completely shrunk, and that they only excised the residue that remained!

*Birmingham 1988*

It was always a delight to go to the farm in Yorkshire, and have wonderful fellowship with Thomas and Jean during Convention times.

We had arranged to go to Keswick Convention in the summer of 1988, before going on to London for the second week of our holiday. Oh, the delight on the Saturday night, praising God and meeting beautiful people, but on the Sunday morning, I felt so unwell that I said to Duncan, "I am either taking a stroke or we are in the wrong place!" On reflection, I do not really know why I said this. After some deliberation and prayer, we packed our bags and headed south. The further away we went, the better I felt. So, "Where do you want us Lord?" was the question uppermost in our minds. Like the best of husbands, Duncan said, "This better be right. I only hope you know what you are doing!"

Passing through Manchester, we soon approached Birmingham, and on the lampposts were posters displaying 'NEC Convention, Speaker: Reinhard Bonnke'. This was a name unfamiliar to us, but as the rain was pouring down, we thought we would call in and see what it was about – at least get a B&B for the night. The receptionist misheard me, and thought I had said to book us in for 'six' nights instead of just 'one' night. However, we joined the queue for the first meeting – powerful, anointed, exciting! We were in the right place! If we had any doubts, they were dispelled when we finally arrived at the B&B house. A lovely Irish lady opened the door to us, we must have looked a strange sight – tired, soaking wet, but saturated in the Spirit of God! "Come on in and get your supper", were the first most welcoming words. When we were introduced to the husband, he said, "Oh, you're Scottish laddie, do you know of a place called Irvine?" Did we not! The conversations went on all week as we sat at the foot of the Master and soaked up every anointed word. The praise was truly awesome with Chris Bowater singing 'Here I am, wholly available' and a host of other anointed praisers and worshippers. Inspired, fired up and blessed out of our socks! What an honour to be invited to be in God's perfect will and enjoy the excitement of being led by the Holy Spirit of Promise!

On the last evening of the Convention, Friday 22 July 1988, after an amazing evening of powerful ministry, Reinhard Bonnke called for Pastors to come out, by nation, to be delivered from the fear of man. As the United Kingdom is near the end of the alphabet, we had a long wait. Towards the end of the line of people, it was announced that the hall had to be evacuated shortly, due to fire regulations. We pressed in there desperate for God's blessing and were almost the last to be prayed for. As soon as the man of God prayed for us, we knew that the Lord had done a mighty work and so we walked out of that arena a free man and a free woman! It was more than a red-letter day or week; it was the turning point in our walk with God for the rest of our lives. Seek Him, and He will make a way to make you whole. I thank God for the leading of the Blessed Holy Spirit.

We came back to the work that God had called us to establish in the Emmanuel Christian Centre in Irvine, full of faith, energy, empowerment and vision!

### *Full-time at the centre*

I continued to serve the Lord in a full-time capacity for a year at the Centre, teaching the Word, visiting, encouraging many people who felt they had lost their way, and also carrying out administration work, while Duncan continued to work full-time in the school. However, a day came in June 1989, when another dream-vision was given to Duncan. In it, he saw himself taking down the keys of his room and telling the Headmaster that he was resigning, and going into the work of the Emmanuel Christian Centre full-time. One month later, it happened, just as he saw in the dream.

Duncan's parents were none too pleased when they discovered that he had given up his 'good job'. However, what they did *not* know was that we had no regular income, but trusted God for all things! He never once let us down, what a mighty God we serve!

After seven years of comfort in the premises on the High Street, we heard that the building was to be sold in the New Year of 1991. Consternation and questions arose. Where would we go? We had no money in the bank as such, but we believed the God who had led us thus far was able to lead in the future. We had proved Him too many times as the great 'I AM' to be downcast or without hope for long.

We got down to more serious prayer and fasting, trusting all the while that God had a better and greater plan for us. What with two Pastors working full-time, a small congregation, little cash, only a few of the Team Members in full-time employment, we had the greatest challenge ahead of us as the Emmanuel Christian Centre Fellowship.

One Friday night during prayer, Pastor Duncan left the meeting and came back with this report:

> There is not a single church open in Irvine tonight. Every church is locked – some even padlocked. I came to the corner of West Road and there was an old church building lying empty, I put my hands on it and said, "Even a place like this Lord, for your Glory"!

Unbeknown to us, the owner of that building had wanted to sell it. A local group of religious people had had the keys for eleven weeks and were still deliberating a price.

Twelve years previously, Reverend Bob Lesley – the last minister of that same old Relief Church – had telephoned to speak to Duncan. However, at that time, Duncan was in Dunoon on business, and we had packed to go on holiday in two days' time. We therefore agreed that Duncan would return the call when we returned. Unfortunately, when we returned home, we read of the sudden death of the Rev. Bob Lesley, and so we will never know for sure what was on Bob's mind. But, "all things work together for good…" (Romans 8:28).

We found that the owner of the old church was a Mr. Wallace. He owned the front part, and the British Legion owned and used the back area.

*Moody and Sankey.*

It is reported that Moody and Sankey preached and sang in this church building while in Irvine in 1891. Revival broke out in the town as the great D L Moody preached the immutable word of God, and Ira Sankey sang the sweet songs of Zion to a captive audience. What a privilege it must have been to have heard him sing:

> I've found a friend in Jesus, He's everything to me, He's the fairest of ten thousand to my soul, The " lily of the valley" in Him alone I see, All I need to cleanse and make me fully whole.

He was voted as being America's number one gospel singer in his time.

*Preparing to move*

It was an overcast, damp January morning, when Duncan and I went to view the building at 2 West Road. At first sight, it looked like a glorified builder's yard, with pieces of old junk strewn about the floor, an air of decay, musty old pews, broken windows, and a dismal, dark, dull, gallery overhead.

Only God could impart faith for a place like this – or, as someone was overheard to comment, "only a mad Pentecostal would take on a place like that!" 'That place' was originally the Relief Church of Scotland, and at one time, it was one of the loveliest buildings in Irvine, but they had vacated the building some twelve years previous and built a new church in the Bourtreehill area of Irvine. For those twelve years, it had lain empty!

We did not have great business acumen, but we did have great faith in a great God! The next week, we took the Team of thirty people to view the building. Some could not see what we saw by way of potential, but the building was so strategically placed that we could not have imagined anything that fitted so well with the call we believe God had given to us for an end-time, apostolic, multi-purpose centre for His people and the community.

As we stood at the back of the gallery, the Lord spoke ever so strongly to me, "If you allow the other party to get this, My House, the Holy Spirit of God will be grieved". I told Duncan about this, and he had no qualms about going after it for God's work. He saw the tremendous potential and even at that moment was drawing up plans in his head as to how it would look when renovated and completed. We asked the Team Members if they were in agreement with us, and would stand by us in the purchase, the renovation, and the hard work involved in the years ahead, plus all the upheaval of moving. All agreed. We could proceed with the project.

Sadly, as happens in all great works, some left, others fell by the wayside, and the faith of others failed, but no gain can be achieved by going into detail at this time in the history of the Emmanuel Christian Centre. God knows all, and He is the righteous judge. Nevertheless, others went on to fulfil their calling in Christ for their lives, and God is blessing in different spheres of ministry. To God be all the glory.

### *Keys handed over on 11 February 1991*

The owner 'liked the look of our faces', and decided to sell it to us for the sum of £25,000. But, the sum that the Lord had given to Duncan and me was £20,000! The purchase price had to be handed over within a few months, so we signed on the dotted line! We were in possession of the keys of 2 West Road church building and had occupancy of it on 11 February 1991. What rejoicing! What celebration! The family thought we were crazy taking on an old building like that, but at that time, they did not know that the ways of God are past finding out! *"He reveals His ways to Moses but His acts to the children of Israel" (Psalm 103:7).*

Removal day came – cold but dry, praise the Lord! How and where were we going? It had to be incognito – across the High Street, through Short's Bakery close, the bigger items down Chapel Lane, across the car park and through the ancient heavy brown church door to set up our 'Tent of Meeting' under the gallery of the old church.

It was Sunday, the streets were quiet and the church services were all underway. Tentatively, the organ, tambourines, curtains, carpets, bookcases, books, Communion Table, were all carried from 152 High Street to 2 West Road and conveniently placed 'in situ'. Duncan had asked for the soon-to-be-discarded wood from the Shopping Mall floor – which was going to be thrown out anyway – to be thrown our way. This would be used to partition the 'Sanctuary' area from the rest of the building. It must be said here, my husband never lost an opportunity to help save money, which could be best kept for the more important materials.

Hastily, the old, grey-corded carpet was stapled down, and the fireproof curtains (from the local hospital, which was about to close down) adorned the walls. The old, blue plastic chairs were tidily put in rows; we turned the temporary lights on and we were as happy as the angels in heaven! To us, it was the greatest cathedral in Britain – after we lit the 'Calor' gas stoves! That morning, we sang our hearts out at the goodness of our God. We had our 'own place' at last, how we appreciated every corner of that old building! At times, we could hardly contain our joy.

The history of the founding of the Emmanuel Christian Centre has been written so that those who follow will never forget the roots, hardship, cost or the faith needed for such a project, and also to 'tell it as it was' for future generations.

Truly, 'Emmanuel' God was with us, and we felt His Presence in a special way. This was no ordinary walk or calling – God challenged us every day and in many ways.

The Sisters of Darmstadt, Germany, were invited to come and speak in the winter of 1991. What grace and beauty was seen as they gently ministered in the power of the Spirit. They loved our dusty old church and shared how they too built the 'Land of Canaan' out of old bricks and stones, after the war when Darmstadt had been raised to the ground with the bombing. Before they left the Centre, we were all given a lovely card with words that Mother Basilea Schlink had written. My card proved to be invaluable to me personally in the walk of faith that I would face in the future. It stated simply: *look to god for help, and you will lack nothing.*

Years later, Duncan and I had the privilege of visiting 'Canaan' in Germany, and were thrilled to walk the grounds and see the mighty hand of God in everything. We met lovely people whose lives were totally dedicated to the call of God. A sister lived here who originally came from Kilmarnock, and she was particularly pleased to meet us as we also came from Ayrshire, Scotland.

One fine day, whilst in Germany, we hired bicycles and took the scenic route to a town ten miles away, through a forest, in order to visit a missionary from Sudan, named Uti, who was on furlough. She had a few days holiday and took us in her car to visit places of historical interest, and of course taste the local food.

While we were away one of the members, (Margaret) wrote the following poem:

## *Be Thou My Vision*

Duncan and Greta – broken free
Gone on a flight to Germany
To see a vision from the Father's heart
Built by wee nun's hands in Darmstadt
With nothing but prayer, faith and grit
A phoenix rose up from the dirt
To show the world what God can do
Using ordinary people like me and you.

Back home, the physical work continued in the building. Old foundations had to be torn out and new foundations laid, as the old church floor was on a downward slant from back to front. This was a mammoth task, and necessitated digging down a good few feet. There was great camaraderie, fun and jokes in abundance as well as plenty of tea, as it could be cold and dusty working in the 'bowels of the earth' – or so it seemed! At the end of the day, we were all tired but happy. As the men were working, the women would gather for prayer. God's answers are far too many to mention.

### *Miracles are on the way*

At one point during this particular task, Duncan came home looking like a miner and said, "Greta, we need a mountain of chip scaling, or fine rubble to fill in the new foundations, and I don't know where it is going to come from!" One thing we did know, God had promised that He would build His House; we were to be obedient and do the work.

The day came when we could not go on with the task, until the scaling was ordered, paid for and delivered. The money had run out, but we had a battery of prayer warriors who were praying 'the next need in'! One day, the foreman of the company that was building a new car park opposite the church called Duncan into his office and explained that, in order to complete the top end of the car park area, he had ordered four tons of scaling, but, lo and behold, the company had sent 40 tons by mistake! As he could not return the balance, was there any way that we could use 36 tons of scaling? Could we not!! Thank you Lord! Great celebrations on a mighty deliverance once again!

We called it God's Mighty Provision! For those who were not with us from 1992 onwards, those were the most exciting days! We prayed, God moved, and the job was done to His praise and glory! Those members of our group who were not in secular work came and crushed cans for scrap metal. One of the men even built a can-crushing machine to make the job easier! Others washed cars at £1 a time; some gave jewellery, all to enhance the 'Building Fund'.

On most Saturdays, there was a hive of industry going on – preparing, stripping lath off walls, brushing up and clearing away. During this time, we had one second-hand, dark blue, (at times) dysfunctional toilet for about thirty people! Somehow, everyone survived the ordeal.

However, the biggest fight of faith was just ahead of us. It is just as well that God often hides the future from us; otherwise, we would never attempt anything.

Dear reader, we were under no illusion regarding the enormity of the work ahead – the financial cost, as well as the physical and family cost. Most people who came in to 'visit' just looked, and one could see by their expression exactly what they were thinking, But we had heard from God to build Him an apostolic, multi-purpose, end-time Centre for His Glory. No matter what the cost, we set our faces as flint (as it were) towards our Jerusalem. We made every day count, and experienced an abundance of His joy, glory and bountiful provision.

The way God worked with Duncan and me was in this way: I would say, "Duncan, did the Lord speak to you during the night?" Some of the most thrilling revelations came then, as words unfolded as how to go about the next part of the work. When Duncan came home, he would say, "Have you had any Divine appointments today, Greta?" Sometimes, it was "Oh yes!", and sometimes "Not really". To have an intimate relationship with the Holy Spirit is the most exciting life as a Christian.

Very early one morning, Duncan got up, and said he felt impressed to go to West Road church, prepare the gallery for demolition but to buy a £5 saw, cut the joists and keep the old pine wood, which would come in handy to make the doorposts and lintels in the months to come. The Lord had spoken to him in a dream. That same week, a businessman from Perth called in to see what was going on in the old church and took a liking to the horseshoe-shaped gallery. He bought it that very afternoon for £400 and it now sits in place of honour in a mansion house in Perthshire. The beautiful, dark oak horse-shoe-shaped gallery had to be removed, as the plans God had given us were to have the 'sanctuary' upstairs and the multi-purpose areas downstairs at ground level. Sometimes, God works quickly when He has a plan. All the joists, which supported the old gallery, were cut and tied up in bundles ready to be dressed later and made into the doorposts, which we now pass through every weekend without further thought!

All this time of working, worshipping, planning and praying – family, friends and people in the town said it could never be finished! "What a black hole". What had we got ourselves into? "Fanatics and fools". We actually felt quite sorry for the sceptics, as only the visionaries can see the vision complete. We had received a mandate from God, and whatever it took, His will, plan and purpose would be accomplished. We were often reminded by the local people that three different local denominations had been offered the building, but all three declined as they felt it was in too great a state of disrepair and that it would cost too much to renovate.

## *God's price*

How did we manage to buy it, and where did the money come from? The owner's price was £25,000, to be paid within a given time. Nothing wrong with that, but Duncan kept saying that it was not God's price. We went along with the original price for some time, but the money was just not coming in. In just over one year, from February 1991 to May 1992, all that came in to buy the property was £7,500! We were disappointed, but I remember the morning that Duncan said, "I have to telephone the owner and ask him to reduce it to God's price of £20,000, and the money will come in"! "All right", was the reply from the other end of the telephone, "But I'm giving you nine weeks to get the balance of the purchase price, because I need the money"! Well, if that was said to us today (Wednesday 7th February 2008, almost 17 years later to the day), would we still have the same faith?

We had to begin praying in earnest so that God would open the windows of Heaven. We stormed heaven until we were hoarse, sang praises night after night, fasted, worshipped and confessed sin. Money came pouring in from interested parties in five pounds, ten pounds, fifty pounds, cheques etc., until, after eight weeks, there was £10,000 in the kitty! One week to go! What excitement – £2,500 still outstanding, surely, the Lord would not let us down at the last minute.

It was D-day weekend (June 1992) before the Tuesday when the owner had to have the purchase price paid in full – or it would revert back to £25,000. We not only prayed, we fasted and prayed again. By faith, two ladies in the Centre ordered a cake with candles to celebrate the balance of £12,500 being handed over that week! Emotions were running high, and the atmosphere was charged with great excitement!

That Saturday, the telephone rang. Friends from Glasgow were interested to know how the project was coming along. My reply was, "very well", as that morning, a cheque for £500 had arrived in the post from a person unknown to us who lived on the island of Arran – which left a balance of £2,000. We rejoiced together!

The telephone rang again a few minutes later from the same friends saying that they had some money laid aside for a 'rainy day', and would be willing to loan us the money to pay the purchase price in full. Immediately, the words tumbled out of my mouth, "Thank you, but by faith the money is in my hand and God will honour His word by demonstrating His almighty power". "Oh", came the reply, "When you get it, let us know. You've got great faith". I assured the lady that she would be the first to know.

The reader must understand here, that at the very beginning of the work, the Lord gave us a scripture through a friend from another church in the town, from the book of Proverbs Chapter 22 verse 7 "*The rich rules over the poor and the borrower is a servant to the lender*". Therefore, we had to grasp the principle quickly that God had instructed us through His Word never to borrow or consider lottery money, as He would touch peoples' hearts to plant a seed into the work, which would bring a harvest in due season if we believed. And just as He had promised, as we looked to Him for help we would lack NOTHING.

Next day was Sunday – worship and praise to the King of Kings and thanksgiving for all His goodness and mercy, but above all, for sending Jesus to be our Saviour Redeemer. The service continued towards its completion, when suddenly, a lady in the back row stood up. She said that she had been asked to come to the Emmanuel Christian Centre that morning, in order to find out what the balance of the purchase price for the building was. Whatever the amount, a cheque would be given for the

Signing for title deeds and celebration time!

Duncan pouring over the plans

outstanding amount by 6 o'clock that evening! On hearing that it was £2,000, she still insisted that whatever the outstanding amount, it would be met that evening, because the people concerned were going on holiday the next day, and felt it necessary to meet the need without delay. There was no end to the songs of praise and Hallelujahs! It was agreed that the celebration cake would be cut on Tuesday evening, accompanied by testimonies of thanksgiving and rejoicing! True to their word, a cheque was handed to us at the end of the evening service.

Duncan and I just looked at one another with tears rolling down our cheeks. We held hands and thanked the Lord who had called us, whose name is Faithful and True. He had done it! He had touched people's hearts, and through their obedience, the first big hurdle had been overcome. He had proved to us that this was His will, and whatever the future held, He would remain steadfast.

Tuesday morning arrived bright and clear, but with no sign of the owner coming to collect the outstanding balance of £12,500 in cash! Had he forgotten? We did rejoice that evening with joy unspeakable and full of glory. Great anticipation filled the air – no debt, the church building was ours, although a lot of hard work lay ahead for us all, plus more faith to believe for finance for the on-going renovation work.

The owner appeared the Thursday morning, looking rather apprehensive. Duncan caught his mood and agreed, "Yes, these were days when there was not a lot of money around and many people we knew were unemployed etc. etc." His face became more and more downcast, as he, being a businessman, needed collateral that very week. Suddenly and unexpectedly, Duncan told him, "But we have the money – God was true to His word. it's all here!" We signed on the dotted line and the Title Deeds were handed over! The owner could not believe that we had got £12,500 in nine weeks and said, "That's some God you've got" – and we agreed wholeheartedly!

The main, very large lintel was rotten, and because we had kept our word and God was faithful, Mr Wallace (the previous owner) offered to get it taken out and a steel one inserted in its place (that in itself was worth over £1,000!) We kept in contact, and he was a good help to us in the initial years of renovating the building.

Plans, plans and more plans! Visits galore to Building Control offices and the Planning Department of Cunninghame District Council. It was said, and I do not know to this day how true it is, that Duncan MacDonald's name will go down in the Guinness Book of Records for the most visits to the local Council Offices to have plans passed, to convert a 200-plus-year-old derelict church building, which had lain empty for twelve years into a modern, two-story, multi-purpose Christian Centre for the community.

Nobody, but nobody in these offices believed it could be done. Anyway, where was the money coming from? Opinions were bandied about hard and fast. Ferocious and wild were the speculations even among the 'best of Christians' in the town, and surrounding area. "They'll never do it". "Too much involved". Relentless and as cruel as the sea, the comments came battering against us. It seemed at one point that everyone had 'Pastors' for dinner!

## *The day the plans were passed*

One fine morning in October 1993, we woke up to the birds chirping, and we sang our favourite song "This is the day that the Lord has made, let us rejoice and be glad in it!" When we felt that we had nothing much to be glad about, it seemed to inject us with faith, just as the Psalmist David had been 3,000 years ago! This was to be a day with a difference – only at the time, we did not know it.

In the evening, we were scheduled to attend a meeting in Glasgow where Morris Cerullo was billed to speak, but Duncan came home quite tired, and did not feel like going. Being the good, encouraging helpmate, I quipped, "Perhaps after a quick shower, you may feel better; and just perhaps, the Lord will speak to your heart and encourage you". His reply was that of someone who had tried and tried again with nothing much apparently happening. Had he really heard from God to build Him a house for His Glory in the middle of the town? Was it 'pie in the sky'? At times, we felt we had been thrown into God's melting pot, and someone was stirring us round and round with no let up.

However, after a quick shower, Duncan came downstairs looking like a million dollars, complete with collar, tie and aftershave. But he said, "God doesn't speak personally any more Greta. Anyway, when I do go out for prayer, the Speaker usually goes the opposite way to where I am standing, and I go back to my seat feeling rather let down".

We headed up to Glasgow and into the City Halls. It was a challenging meeting, and our faith had started to rise again. At about 9 o'clock, Pastors were called to come out if they desired prayer. I said, "Let's go!" He said, "No". I replied, "We've got nothing to lose; let's go!" pushing him out in front of me. There we stood, in one long straight line. Yes, the man of God did go to the other end of the line – but we held hands and prayed, trusting God all the way.

Unexpectedly, Morris Cerullo turned on his heel, and came straight towards us, and with tears streaming down his face simply said, "The plans have been passed today! Take courage and build. The way will not be easy, but do that which God has spoken to you!" He moved on without a backward glance. No other words needed to be spoken at that Divine moment – it is absolutely true that things of earth grow strangely dim in the light of His Power and Presence!

I do not remember sleeping that night. God had spoken thunderous words of immense magnitude into our minuscule orld that in years to come would make all the difference between hell and Heaven! This to us was surely an encounter of the God-kind!

The next day did not come quickly enough – Planning Department was high on the agenda. Walking with the air of a king, Duncan strode into the precinct of Cunninghame District Council – with a secret in his heart from the Throne Room of Heaven itself!

"I am delighted to tell you, Mr MacDonald, that the plans to enovate the church at 2 West Road were passed at 3 p.m. yesterday afternoon". Surprise, surprise!

What a mighty God we serve. No one, just no one, compares with Him. The Fellowship erupted when we called a special meeting to tell them the good news. Now, we really could go to town, roll up our sleeves and pull up our socks, no place for wimps or wallies here! All put their hand to the plough and we were on our way.

*The move is on*

By this time, we had vacated our makeshift, temporary accommodation of polythene, old carpets, curtain-lined walls, Calor gas stoves – our 'tabernacle in the wilderness'. We rather reluctantly put our old, blue plastic chairs into cold storage until we could use them again, whenever that might be. From there, we moved on to the Templars' Hall and then the Guide Hall in Muir Drive. We had a very successful Christmas Sunday School Party, followed by a season of wonderful fellowship with each other and with the visiting speakers who continued to come and encourage us on our journey.

It was time to move on once more, but to where? We felt like the children of Israel without a permanent dwelling, but we had the assurance that one day, we would be back in 2 West Road, and enter our 'Promised Land'. The Vision would be completed.

Our next port of call was the village of Springside. The district in which the church was situated was very rough and soon became known as 'Apache land'. Sometimes, the slates were being pulled off the roof and the door banged as we worshipped! Nevertheless, God was still moving by His mighty power – the church was packed most Sundays, and there was great interest in the Word of God.

One of the member's mother died (Maisie by name), and Duncan agreed to officiate at the funeral. The next week Maisie's husband Gil came to the meeting, and was deeply impressed by the welcome, the service and the love shown to him. Gil made up his mind to get right with God and to make peace with his Maker. The following week, he came forward for salvation, held out his two hands and said, "I offer them to you, take me Lord, as I am". Duncan now had another faithful servant who worked tirelessly day after day establishing the renovation and the building-up of the work in West Road. He grew in faith and remained faithful to the end.

At about this time, Brian came from the 'Job Creation Scheme', and worked for two years; then he came back voluntarily when his time was up with the Government scheme. He was with us or another year, until some misguided person informed the relevant office, and said he was being paid, which was not the case. Brian worked on because, as he said to me personally at a later date, the best years of my life were when I worked with Duncan" – with meaning in his voice, as tears formed in his eyes.

In Springside Mission Hall, there was a baptismal tank, so we made good use of it and a goodly number of folk were baptised, including Gil, Wendy, Adam and Elaine.

We moved on yet again – we became really good at flitting, and taking the minimum of stuff with us. As long as we follow the Glory cloud, we feel safe and secure in His love!

The Emmanuel Christian Centre congregation arrived one bright Sunday morning to worship in the back hall of the congregational Church in Dreghorn, about four miles from Irvine. The rental as £40 per month for the use of the wooden structure four times a week. We were getting closer to our final destination.

As well as the venue being changed time after time, we, as a congregation, were also being changed and challenged, as Bible Studies were well attended by all the Team Members.

Once again, we were blessed and knew that God was with us also in our next move. One never-to-be-forgotten Sunday morning, there was a particular anointing for words of knowledge (as found in 1 Corinthians 12:8).

We had reached the height of glory in the time of worship and praise to the only wise and living God, when Duncan, the servant of the Lord, moved into words of prophecy, wisdom and knowledge. Towards the end of this mighty out-pouring of the Spirit of the Lord came a revelation that there was someone who had had a bad experience a few years previously, which had left the person with a great fear. God wanted to remove that fear that morning. No one answered. However, a member's husband, who had come for his wife to run her home, was standing in the porch, behind the glass door. To our amazement, he was the person whom the Holy Spirit was speaking about, and he was invited to be brave and come forward as God wanted to remove the fear from him. Although he did not understand any 'holy' or 'religious' ways, he knew that after prayer, God had mightily touched him that morning.

He then told his story. A few years earlier, he had been under the engine of a car that had not been properly jacked up. Suddenly, the whole engine of the car fell on his chest, and he had been reliving his ordeal for the last few years. God removed his fear, because He is no respecter of persons – that young man had not been at 'church' that morning, but God met him at the point of his need and took away his fear. What a mighty, kind and compassionate God we serve. As we often sing, "There is no God like Jehovah!"

After 18 months in Dreghorn, Duncan and I were beginning to feel restless, when the Lord began to speak to us again. One evening, Duncan came home having had a disappointing day. People had not turned up as scheduled to help, and he felt this keenly, because it hindered the progress of the renovation. We retired to bed with pensive minds and inquiring hearts. "Lord, just what are You saying? Please help, we have been here so many times, and there seems to be so many delays and denials. Are we really doing Your will, are we in Your Plan 'A' for our lives? Did we miss hearing from You?" So many unanswered questions. Deep, deep down, we did have a settled peace above the turmoil. One of the mottos for a previous year was "*By him actions are weighed*" (1 Samuel 2:3), and a more recent one, "*He is faithful that promised*" (Hebrews 10:23). We clung to the Lord of God like a vice and reminded Him often of His immutable, changeless nature.

*A holy trek*

Surprisingly and clearly, we knew it was time to embark on a holy trek in order to clear our minds and take stock. No mistake about where to go. This time, we were to take several crosses that Duncan had hand-made, and travel northwest. We were to plant them in the heather, the soil, rock, sand, sea and the place where the Scottish Kings and Queens were crowned, last but not least, in the private chapel in the grounds of the estate where Rees Howells viewed the parchment with the names of the Covenanters scratched in blood.

Sunday morning came, and off to church we went with our car loaded and ready for the trip. There was great anticipation in the air – the congregation were fully behind us. They knew that when we returned, we would have exciting tales to tell of the mightiness of God in His leading and how He would undertake for every need. There was great joy as we left; we felt so privileged to be loved and cared for. The family of God is a very precious thing in these days of great uncertainty.

There were two books that never left my bedside table in those days – one was 'Realities' by Basilea Schlink, which inspired us greatly. 'Realities' is the story of how God brought cosmos out of chaos after the bombing of Darmstadt (Germany) during the war. Mother Basilea knew that she had heard from God to 'build a land of Canaan' from the bombed-out debris of the town with the help of the Sisters she taught in Bible Class.

Her vision came to pass after many years, with many setbacks and heartaches along the way. We had the honour and privilege of staying there, at Canaan in the late 1990's. For us, it was a dream come true – to walk into someone else's realised vision! It gave us hope and renewed our vigour. The Sisters were so kind, understanding and interesting.

The second book was 'Intercession' by Rees Howells. It was equal to 'Realities' in faith, despite the great odds stacked against the author. The unerring, unswerving faith of Rees Howells, as he fought for truth, challenges every reader who opens the page to engage on a gigantic journey of the real supernatural order. The God of Rees Howells was real and very much alive, up-to-date, and constantly planning great things for those "*who had an ear to hear what the Spirit was saying to the church*". In these end-times, that means you and me!

These writings were so penned that we both could glean and gain much from their God-ordained experiences. We shall hear more of Rees Howells as God unfolds His directive for our lives.

We were just about to embark on our mission of purpose to the northwest, when one of the sisters from the Fellowship said, “I would like you to have this frozen chicken and some potatoes, they may come in handy”. Obediently, we thanked her, and put them in the boot of the car without another word.

Goodbyes having been said, we drove off with a sense of real excitement in our spirits. How wonderful to be in the centre of God’s will and be as happy as we were! We wrote a Journal about our experiences that unfortunately got lost in the mists of time, but some of the photographs have been unearthed – which is good for posterity sake.

Highlights of the journey have been etched in my memory and will be so for eons of time to come – such as the unforgettable orange-red sunset reflected on the mirror-like water as we approached Arisaig in the North West Highlands. It is a sight that I shall never forget, but the traffic behind us made it impossible to stop and take a photograph of this glorious ethereal vision of yet another facet of God’s timeless handiwork.

As evening was upon us, it was time to book into a Bed & Breakfast for the night. We liked the look of the imposing house on the hill that complied with the budget, so booked in, and went to our room for the night.

The Lord spoke words into our spirits in the watches of the night, which we shared with the saints when we returned home. But these whispers from the Lord were for those times past, to encourage the saints at that time ever onward and upward. We would be wise to remember how God, through the Holy Ghost, encouraged us in ways of physical and spiritual restoration so that in the dark, dangerous and often difficult days ahead, we would be saved from going back and falling by the wayside. He often speaks to warn of dangers ahead – it is to our advantage to take note and apply His correction in the day of His favour.

In the morning, after breakfast, we loaded up to continue our journey northwards, when I remembered the now defrosted chicken, and potatoes, in the boot of the car. What were we to do with them? There was nowhere for us to cook them, and we did not want the chicken to spoil. On the spur of the moment, when paying the bill to the lady of the house, I offered her the fresh food. "Well, well, well, that's strange", she said. "My 90-year-old mother said that she had not had roast chicken and potatoes for weeks because the road to Mallaig was under repair and Morag couldn't get to the big supermarket. We have had to put up with 'junk food' until the road is opened up again! God has answered our prayer; it will be a lovely roast meal tonight for dinner!" We were happy to hand over the food, and they were delighted to receive it.

*Planting of the first cross*

Do not question God when He asks you to do one or two things that you do not understand at the time. His Word says: "*Obedience is better than sacrifice*" (1 Samuel 15:22).

Driving over a rough track road seaward, we came across thick bell-heathers, masses of embankments of gorgeous strong shades of deep lilacs plunging into dark purples. It is here that we first stopped and gave thanks to God the Creator of the sun, sea and sky for His bountiful provision in the gift of nature. What a feast for the eyes – what wondrous beauty on the earth!

As we prayed together and read the eternal truth of the Word of God, we were very conscious of an invisible host around us at that moment as we placed the foot high hand-made cross in the denseness of the heathers at Rhu that first morning.

Then we were on the move again, with no time to lose in the work of the Lord. We understood with a fresh realisation that many years ago, the heather had been stained with the blood of the Covenanters in this our beloved land of Scotland. We openly repented before a Holy God for all the atrocities and battles that had been fought and lost, in the name of religion! We asked our precious Redeemer, the Lord Jesus Christ, to cleanse our land and visit our shores with His Calvary love, forgiveness and peace.

Oh the deep, deep joy of knowing Him. "*Oh that I might know Him and the power of His resurrection*", dare we add, "*and the fellowship of His sufferings, being conformed to His death*" (Philippians 3:10).

We had a long journey ahead, as the road to Inverness and the farthest north-point is very narrow and winding. We sang as we drove along, and had Divine encounters on the way, taking every opportunity to give a tract, or speak a word for the Master. We prayed for the folks back home that God would keep them in His love. Everyone that God entrusted to us was and is very precious. The old enemy is never ever far away, and to be forewarned is to be forearmed.

Dunrobin Castle, Sutherlandshire looked inviting for tea and biscuits. It was wonderful to stretch our legs and have a walk around the beautiful grounds with the defiant North Sea waves pounding off the rocky walls. The poet was never more accurate when he penned the words – time and tide wait for no man!

Our next port of call was John o' Groats. We were a bit jaded by this time, so we just felt like climbing up onto the biggest chair in Scotland and having a 10-minute nap!

Duncansby Head, the most northerly point in Scotland – what a rugged yet majestic scene unfolded before our eyes.

Not another human being in sight – only the occasional squawking of the grey gull could be heard, and the gentle lapping of the pale blue water as it kissed the land.

In days gone by, Vikings with their raiding ships swept up these unspoilt shores, cruel and ruthless, setting fire to the peaceful land after ill-gotten gain and much plundering. But not today, this was the day when a wooden cross was buried deep in the sand to remind principalities and powers that Jesus' blood avails to conquer every foe. He is victor over all enemies who would dare oppose His great end-time plan for our beloved land of the thistle, the bluebell and the heather – our Scotia! With tears and many battles, our ancestors fought and won freedom at great cost. We also must hold up the banner of the Cross of Christ who alone brings true freedom, with dignity and pride.

The night was dark, and it was 9 o'clock. We had driven down to the Black Isle, and now it was time to find a place to stay the night. On either side of the road on which we had parked was a B & B house. Which one? You go to the right and I will go to the left and see which is the most suitable. Only one person at home – Effie McKenzie, and she had a comfortable little bungalow, and yes, there was room for us. In the morning after breakfast, she asked where we were off to next, and we told her that it was a 'holy trek' upon which we had embarked. She was very interested to  now our story. After some time speaking about the ways of God, she asked if anyone could know for sure whether they were going to heaven. We explained the way of salvation to her, and led her in the sinner's prayer right there and then. She replied, "I have been waiting all my life to hear what you have just told me, and I go to church every Sunday. Thanks for knocking at my door". We told her that Jesus had been knocking at her heart's door for a long time, and that morning, she had opened her whole being to Him and let Him in. It had been so easy to share the Gospel with Effie. Salvation is only a prayer away. What a farewell, as we told her that if we did not see her again in this life, we would certainly see her in heaven.

The heather, the sand and now, the next place to plant a Cross –

in the cleft of the rock. Cruden Bay was the next port of call – we were enjoying this holy trek more than words can tell. Through placing the crosses in strategic places, we were reminding hell that the victory was won at the cross of Calvary over 2000 years ago, and that His blood still avails and cries out effectually from the ground. Apart from the Lord Jesus Christ and His shed blood, life is meaningless, hopeless, full of chaos. Sadly, many people live unfulfilled lives. Some are so caught up in the roundabout of materialism that they never fully realise the reason for their birth.

Suddenly and unexpectedly, the Holy Spirit of Promise will come in all His Majestic fullness and again sweep across our beloved nation in revival power. We believe it; and work, watch and pray towards that goal. "Do it again Lord!" we pray. Joel, chapter two says, "*In the last days I will pour out My Spirit on all flesh*".

Craggy, impressive red rock beckoned us down a narrow winding pathway. On the way to the bay, dotted here and there, were quaint little workers' cottages with whitewashed walls and colourful tubs of late summer flowers in profusion. Sitting outside in the sunshine, three leathery, lined faces of fishermen with nets at their feet having a 'crack', putting the world to rights, all the while sucking on their long-gone-out pipes! At last, we arrived at an inviting spot, away from civilisation and sounds, apart from the crunch of gravel and breaking twigs underfoot. Methinks this must have been a haven for smugglers in the bad old days; little coves and inlets, caves and hidden recesses, a veritable sanctum for contraband, bandits and rum-running racketeers.

Surely, there was a place here, in the cleft of the rock, in which to shelter the wooden cross from the ravages of the elements when the howling winds and driving rain savagely pound against the inlet. There must be an expression of hope to be resurrected in the day of God's visitation on our island and the islands of the sea. It is more than a plain, simple wooden cross. This enactment was decreed in heaven in order to remind principalities and powers that Jesus Christ is Lord over the whole earth, and He will bring His mighty purposes to pass even in Scotland in His time – in the intervening years this precious land is covered by the blood of His Cross, and only what He allows will be. Our God is Sovereign and He is a Covenant keeping God who cannot go back on His Oath!

## *Dunadd Fort*

Where now Lord, to plant a cross in the soil? A seed-thought began to germinate; Duncan's grandparents came from the islands of North and South Uist and settled in Argyllshire around Kilmartin and Bridgend. In the mid 1900's, Aunt Bella and Aunt Nessie ran the local Post Office in the village, and also, with some help, the tailor's business at the back of the shop. It is a well known story that when the crew were filming high up in the local glen that the film stars, including Sean Connery, would come into the Post Office from time to time for stamps, to post a letter, or to hear the latest local news. He was a great favourite with the village folk. In time, Duncan's grandparents moved from the quiet village in the Highlands to the bustling city of Glasgow.

We travelled across country, and Kilmartin was in sight – why did we not remember before? Of course! We were near Dunadd Fort, the hill where the Kings of Dalriada were crowned. A plaque states:

> Dunadd was the capital of the Scots of Dalriada, occupied intermittently from the 6th – 9th Centuries AD. It is an outstanding example of a dark age fortification, every advantage is taken of natural features by stone ramparts, which form a series of defensive enclosures extending from the main citadel on the summit.

Where else to plant a cross in the soil other than where the crowning of the Kings took place hundreds of years ago? Certainly, a place where oaths and covenants were uttered and allegiance given. If only the stones could talk, what tales they would have to tell of victories, bloodshed, rivalry and celebrations! We climbed the hill on a lovely October day at 9.30 in the morning, our hearts and voices singing the praises of the King of all Kings 'Jesus Christ is Lord'.

Pastor Ian Macpherson, one time Principal of the Apostolic Church Bible School in Penygroes, South Wales, preached a most powerful sermon that we never forgot, and often referred to when relating to the creation of our universe – Out of chaos He brought cosmos. Out of the ruins of lives and of nations, He can bring peace and safety, and kingly rule.

That fresh morning, sitting amid the ruinous rock formations in the warm glow of an autumn day, all was well. But in the dark depths of winter's howling winds with its enemies' vengeful armies on the heels of Dalriada's inhabitants, it would be a dark, bloody night indeed. A veritable valley of Baca to the soul. Man's passion for power, domination and glory can be traced back to the Garden of Eden. The world and people have not changed in over 6,000 years. That is why Father God had to send a Saviour, His only Son, the Lord Jesus Christ, to bring humanity back to Himself by way of a cruel Roman rugged cross.

As we descended the hill where great deeds took place, it was with an air of accomplishment having done what was appointed to us that morning. Silently, but pensively we returned to Base Camp from where our travels took us back to the lowlands of Scotland, to the buzz and centre of business-life again. Somewhat reluctantly, we made our way southwest and home to Ayrshire, eager to tell all that the Lord had done on the holy trek.

After a few weeks' break, the call was already in our hearts to continue the quest to visit another three places before our

Dunadd Fort Hill

Where the Kings of Dalriada were crowned

Making a proclamation that Jesus Christ is King of Kings

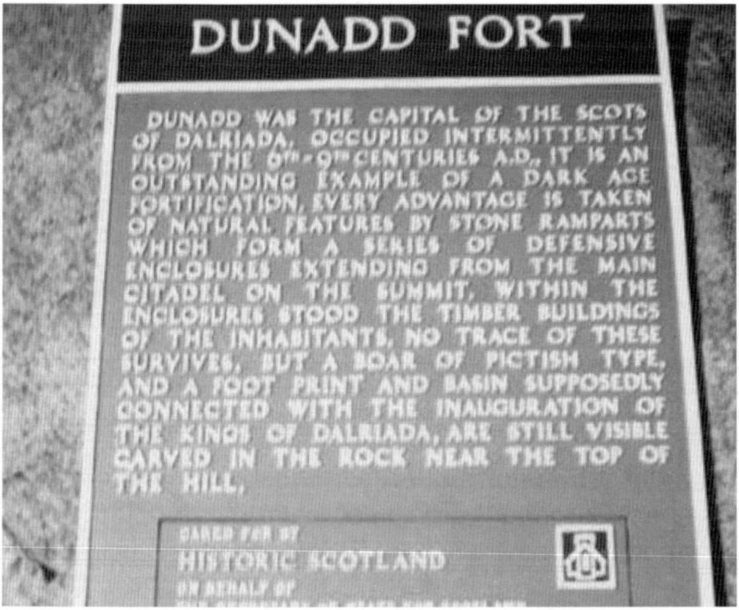

Cardoness House Chapel

odyssey would be complete. The leaves were already turning a burnished bronze and falling to the ground like a patchwork carpet of golds, greens, browns and silver-grey. The day dawned crisp and clear, we were ready with a boot-bulging car, a full tank and rarin' to go!

Our peregrination took us to Holy Island, Lindisfarne. Sacred and holy things indeed happened on this soil. We could feel the breath of God across our cheeks as we walked from 'the Basin' on the west; south to the remains of the Benedictine Priory, past Steel End to the old castle; north east with Bible Law on the left and Brides Hole on the coastline.

Walking due north to Emmanuel Head, we reverently placed the cross in the upstanding plain stones, very conscious that great men and women of God had traversed these places centuries before us, namely Cuthbert, Aiden and Bede.

We retired for the night to a local B&B having wonderful conversations with the other guests One lady in particular was a missionary on furlough from India, enjoying a few days relaxation before going back to answer the call once more to her adopted land. Mugs of hot chocolate helped to thaw us out after the long hike round the island. Tired but happy was the mood of the evening.

### *On the road, again*

The next port of call was something one only dreams about, having read in books about the Scottish Covenanters' tenacity and faith. The question is posed once more today: "Will the real Christians please stand up?"

Crossing over moorland, up hills and down dales, the picture and colour constantly changing in the late autumn sunlight. We had never been to this part of South West Scotland, ever. It was like looking through a kaleidoscope, breathtakingly beautiful!

To pass the time, I picked up the book – 'Rees Howells: Intercessor' by Norman Grubb, and began to read the part where the lady, in whose house Rees was staying for a few days, took him to the front bedroom window and showed him the spot where scores of Covenanters had been martyred for their faith. The following day, they were invited to tea with Sir William and Lady Maxwell at Cardoness House. The first thing he did was to take them to a small room, in which a framed document hung on the wall. He said, "I am going to show you the most precious Deed in Scotland – the Deed signed by the Blood of the Covenanters". Rees said, "When I saw that Deed, the strength of God came into me and changed my body from clay to steel". How we all need an experience like that!

We stopped the car, prayed, and asked the Lord to reveal to us where He wanted us to go next. The map clearly indicated that we were only one-hour's drive from Anwoth! We skirted the parish, not knowing what we were looking for until we came to a sign saying 'Cardoness Estate', marked strictly private! How our hearts beat faster as we drove up the tree-lined driveway not knowing what to expect. An office and reception was before us. We enquired about the Deed and were told that it had been removed a few years earlier, and now hung in one of the galleries in Edinburgh.

Where to plant a cross was on our heart. We asked for permission to walk round the private grounds and this was granted. There was just something different about this place – we walked and talked, walked and prayed, until we came across a little stone chapel built on raised ground overlooking a sandy enclave with the Solway waters ebbing and flowing on a gentle tide. This was like the breath of God to our souls. We knew that many holy men and women of God had prayed in this tiny chapel, and we added our prayers to theirs, and hung the cross on the wall in obedience to what we felt He was saying to us. We also knew that that day God was making a Divine statement to principalities and powers – Jesus Christ is Lord!

*Duncan's crosses*

The reader may well ask, "How did it come about that crosses were made and why put them where you did?"

It was May 1988, when the door to the Technical Room at Prestwick Academy burst open rather abruptly, and a disruptive pupil was ushered in. Duncan was asked to keep the lad busy, as he was having one of his 'off' days! After showing the boy several times how to make the current year's model, and frustrated at his mistakes, the boy threw the wasted pieces of wood into the garbage bin in anger. The reflection on the wall from the wasted wood in the bin as the sun shone in the window was of a large cross! Out of apparent useless effort came something of great worth. Nothing was wasted. Duncan then showed the young boy how to take two pieces of thrown-away waste material and make it into something meaningful. When the cross had been polished and varnished, he gave it to the now very impressed young lad, who went back to his next class having been made to realise that God can take our messed-up life and make something worthwhile and beautiful out of it.

In ten years, literally hundreds of crosses were given away as gifts. They were a great comfort and blessing to people up and down the land. Some had texts on them, such as: "Have faith in God", "He is faithful who promised"; others the 'praying hands' in gold or silver lettering. Anyone who wanted one received one freely.

During the early years of the Emmanuel Christian Centre, people of all denominations, the rich, the poor, some of no affiliation, came to see what was going on. A 'Centre' was a new thing 25 years ago – a place to come and go but not necessarily to join. We were not looking for members, but Spirit-filled people, who were called by God to stay and be part of this vital ministry to the people of Ayrshire, and to serve him in whatever capacity He directed, both with natural and spiritual giftings.

Two incidents stand out in stark contrast. A lovely lady came one Saturday night for prayer and received a healing to her ankle. She was so blessed with the love and openness shown to her that she brought her husband a few weeks later. The time came when they decided to move house, so they put their house on the market for sale. After a few weeks, it still had no buyers, so they moved the advertisement to a more local estate agent where it caught someone's interest. The day came for viewing; the couple concerned liked the house and were taken upstairs. On the wall of the main bedroom hung one of Duncan's crosses and the two parties were delighted to realise that they each knew Duncan and yours truly; they also had a cross at home in one of their rooms! The tale ended in a good Christian sale and the deal was made!

A local minister by the name of John came into the school and from time to time would call into Duncan's room to have a chat. One particular day, he told Duncan that he was very disappointed, as a certain ministry, to which he had applied, had turned him down for the post to lecture on the Gifts of the Holy Spirit. Duncan prayed with him, gave him a cross and counselled him to wait another year and apply again. Time went by and John never appeared until one day, a bouncing, beaming, Spirit-filled man burst into the room holding high an envelope, "I've been accepted! Glory to God, and my family and I move south in three months time!" The text on the cross was, "*When He has tried me, I shall come forth as gold*" (Job 23:10).

A few years passed, and we had been taken to Sussex by a student friend who wanted to show us around the College she was attending. By the time we arrived, the Campus was closed, but we managed to get in through a side door. As we were being escorted round, who should open the main doors but our friend John of years before! Hugs and greetings all round! "Let me take you to my office", he said. When he opened the door, there in front of us was the cross, with the text still intact. Surely, He does know the way that we take, and we rejoice in His leading even though at times we do not understand the delays or why so many battles have to be fought along the road of life!

> N.B. Crosses are symbols of hope that one day God would send revival to our beloved land again, and become torches of living flame, satellites of power!

*The battle is the lord's – not ours!*

During the formative years, God always spoke into our lives either by the Word of Scripture, directly into our heart, or sometimes through a word of knowledge, as found in 1 Corinthians 12:8. It was an unwritten rule that we would not make any blind decisions without the mind of the Holy Spirit on everything.

*The vision will be completed*

As we were interceding before the Lord as a Fellowship, we brought before Him the great need of materials and finances to build up and renovate the structure of the church building within and without. A mighty formidable task lay ahead of us, but we had a prayer in our heart, 'the vision will be completed'. In those early days, Gil and Brian worked tirelessly with Duncan, and great was the comradeship, second to none. 'Big Jim' joined them at a later date.

At about this time, I began to discern the whispers of the Great God and Saviour of mankind – the indescribable omnipotent Father of the entire universe, in the early hours of the morning speak like this: "Because of your obedience to My will, and righteous faith on My call in your life, I will cause people to give into your hands enough substance to clear your mortgage". Thunderous words, could this really be God, how could this possibly happen?

I am no mystic or different from anybody else who has answered the call of God in their life. Millions of people have given up their earthly ambitions to do the will of God because He compels one to follow fully all the way no matter the obstacles.

Normally, I would tell Duncan everything, but this was different, this was thousands of pounds for us personally. Again and again, I heard the whispers of the Lord deep down in my inner being. Could this be true? I was to find out in the weeks and months that ensued. People began to give me money telling me specifically, "This is not for the building, or work of the Emmanuel Christian Centre. The Lord has told me, this is for you; just be blessed!" I do not know to this day the number of people who were moved by God to give in this way. I only know that God was true to His Word, and caused people to hear from Him and give. Some I know, and some I have never met.

Well, I was bowled over at first, then I started to see the greatness of our God in the land of the living. He is true to His Word, and He cannot go back on His Word.

One afternoon, I thought that I would lay out all the money on top of the bed to count it. I did not want to put it into any bank; I just added to the pile what was received with thanks. As I was counting … £1,000, £2,000, £3000, etc., Duncan came quietly upstairs into the bedroom and said, "boo". I nearly jumped out of my skin, as I had not heard him come upstairs, because I was so engrossed in amazement. His first words were, "Have you robbed a bank?" To which I replied, "I can't tell you just now, but at the right time, I'll tell you what this is all about". He was perfectly content with that answer because we trusted one another implicitly in all these things.

The day came when I walked into the Building Society and paid the mortgage in full. No more debt. Owing nothing, what a wonderful feeling! What a mighty God we serve. I was very concerned about money when I left my job, thinking that I had given up so much. A year later, Duncan obeyed the Lord and left his work in the School. Were we mad? Scores of others had done it before us, and God proved faithful. In every area, we have proved the faithfulness of God, and He is no man's debtor. He more than made up to us for all we thought we had lost!

Now I could tell Duncan. "Tonight we are going out to celebrate some very good news". During the meal at our favourite restaurant, Duncan said, "Well tell me, what are we celebrating?" My reply, "We have no mortgage! Remember you saw all the money on top of the duvet … God moved people's heart to give, not for the on-going work of the Centre, but it was to be for us personally. Months ago, I heard the whispers of the Lord say that He would cause this to happen because of our obedience". His eyes were as big as saucers at this latest miracle. We could only bow our heads and thank Him who does all things well. Only the God of gods could have caused this to happen. We will never cease to praise Him!

Without consistent Friday nights of prayer and intercession, the work would never have been completed. Only God and eternity will tell the full story of His leadings in our lives. On many a cold, et, dark Friday night, brave souls would determine, in their spirit, to wend their way to whatever hall we occupied at that time, be it bleak country, village, or town. Many an icy night, the electrifying power of the Holy Ghost would invade suddenly with His tangible Presence, and He would speak to the waiting saints to encourage, exhort, and sometimes warn, thus enabling His people to be forewarned.

Never-to-be-forgotten nights of the Holy Ghost-kind indeed, when He stirred up the dying embers of our faith and determination, making the formidable task look possible! At times, when we thought that we would never make it and the enemy thought to ravage our heart, the mighty Christ would gently whisper and remind us, "The battle is the Lord's!" No matter what the forces of hell would do, we reminded satan that he did not have the last word, God did and it is not over until He says it is over!

## DIVERSE MINISTRIES

### *Prayer box ministry*

In an early 'Newsletter' – October 1984 to be exact – it is recorded that the Emmanuel Christian Centre Prayer Box Ministry was introduced. Many fellowships since that time and over the years have adopted this type of collecting prayer requests for salvation, healing and deliverance, financial needs and family problems. One person is responsible for praying over the requests. There is also an 'answer to prayer' box. An untold number of prayer requests over the years have been answered and we give the glory back to God for answering prayer.

### *Prayer cloth ministry*

This ministry was also introduced at this time. Squares of white cotton are prayed over, anointed with oil, given or sent to the person requesting healing of body, mind or spirit. For one, my mother-in-law (Nana MacDonald) would not go to sleep without the prayer 'contact' for her continued healing and help from the Lord under her pillowslip. Such was her faith in the living Lord.

On one occasion, when the doctor came to visit, the prayer cloth fell out and she explained in full detail to him how in the New Testament (Acts 19:12) the apostle Paul prayed over handkerchiefs and aprons and people were healed. He was impressed, and no doubt, the rest of the surgery personnel heard of this strange phenomenon at the coffee break!

### *Purse ministry*

One lovely warm day, Duncan and I decided to go to Millport on the island of Cumbrae for a few hours break. At that time, he had been talking to me about an array of colours he kept seeing before his eyes – beautiful reds, greens, purples etc. As we walked along the seafront, there, hanging up in one of the shop windows, were small zip-up purses of every colour. "That's just what I've been looking for", Duncan exclaimed. For weeks he had been telling me, how various colours represented various needs in the Body of Christ; e.g. yellow 'salvation'; brown 'baptism of the Holy Spirit'; green 'inner healing', purple a 'miracle' etc.

Here, they were represented in coloured purses. We went into the shop and bought the lot. How excited we were at God's great provision. Now we could go back to the Fellowship and put the Lord's plan into action! It was simply explained like this: "Have you been praying for a loved one to be saved? Do you have faith enough to believe they can be saved? Take a yellow purse and, as a token of sacrifice to the Lord, put into the purse two-pence or even five-pence as you pray in faith believing for that person's salvation". As people took the purses and they filled up, they were emptied at regular intervals and the sum collected given to missionaries, evangelists or help to get a personal ministry off the ground. Even in this, God answered prayer and the Purse Ministry has proven to be a great blessing. It still continues as a source of encouragement to many over twenty years later!

*Biento broadsheets*

One other 'ministry' that cannot be overlooked is the 'Biento' broadsheets. This came into being when we, and a number of Emmanuel Christian Centre members, went to the WEC House at Kilcreggan for a week's holiday in July 1984. A number of missionaries on furlough from different countries were also attending. One evening, during their talk, they told us about tracts or 'broadsheets' that were printed once a quarter and sent to the various nations in Africa and at times further afield. "Would you be interested in sending hope to the hopeless?"

"Yes", we responded. "Let's be His hands and His feet and have a part in this tremendous outreach". Billy and Lilian have continued to count, wrap, address and send these broadsheets for 15 years; Mary did this for the first seven years. Sometimes word comes back of salvation or healing, sometimes there is no word, but we continue to pray and sow the seed in obedience to God's call at that time. It is exciting and encouraging when there is a letter to let us know that the broadsheet has made a special impact on a person's life. In these days, people need the Lord more than ever, and they have to know that someone somewhere really does care. By helping in these small ways, we feel we are bringing people closer to the Lord Jesus Christ and His undying love for a dying world. Billy and Lilian have continued this vital outreach ministry with ever-increasing zeal.

### *Water baptismal services*

From the onset of the work, we encouraged new believers to be baptised in water as laid down in the scriptures. Not having a baptismal tank in any of the halls we rented, with the exception of 'Apache land' – Springside, it was always an adventure to see where we would go to hold a baptismal service, and who we could bless en-route. A few services stand out as being extra special.

One fine Sunday morning, an excited crowd piled into a 56-seater hired bus laden with Bibles, guitars, sandwiches, flasks and loads of goodies. The latest songs and choruses echoed wherever we went. An hour and a half later, we arrived at the little Pentecostal church in the village of Sanquhar in Dumfriesshire, just in time for the morning service. The congregation had been so faithful over the years, but sadly the numbers had dwindled to a handful, so that when we arrived, the overseer thought he would have a convention that morning – great was the enthusiasm and warm was the welcome. After lunch, we continued on to the Leadhills and set up camp for the afternoon. It was a lovely sunny day and not a few went down into the river and were gloriously baptised.

The next day at the local supermarket checkout in Irvine, the cashier quipped, “You enjoyed yourselves yesterday”! We were taken aback and blurted out that we were not at home yesterday. “Oh I know you weren’t – you were at the Leadhills, and were baptising people in the river”! It just goes to prove that wherever you go your testimony follows you – a complete stranger to us saw the witness of the new Christians and was totally blessed.

Springside mission hall had a baptismal tank, wow! A number of believers were desirous of water baptism, so arrangements were made for the big day. Pastors Billy and Bridie were invited to help during the service, along with members of their congregation. The Mission Hall was packed to capacity and the rafters echoed with the glorious praises of God’s people worshipping and magnifying His Wonderful Name! At least six, possibly eight candidates went into the waters of baptism that night. Children surrounded the pool with great delight and entered into the spirit of the service with great enthusiasm, also getting very wet in the process.

On another occasion, we arrived at the village of Luss, a very picturesque village on the banks of the beautiful Loch Lomond, but the weather turned into a very dull, grey day. This did not dampen our enthusiasm, and after a few sandwiches and hot tea, a few people waded out and were baptised with the rain battering down. As Duncan said the prayer, “On the confession of your faith, I baptise you in the name of the Father, the Son and the Holy Spirit”, a shaft of light beamed down on one of the candidates and a great swell of praise went up from those who stood on the beach, including the on-lookers on an otherwise dismal afternoon.

It must be recorded that one very chilly Easter Sunday morning, we made our way to Dunure, in South Ayrshire, down the ‘electric brae’ and into the harbour car park. We had hired the village hall for the candidates to change in, and also to have an evangelistic outreach in the afternoon. After the fifth young man had been baptised, Duncan said he did not have any feeling in his legs, as the waters of the sea were so icy cold! He was teased mercilessly as he struggled to walk back to the shore. Volunteers were lining up to help get some heat into his freezing leg muscles. After some time, all was well, and we continued with praising and worshipping the God of all grace, love and mercy.

We always found a very warm welcome at the Church at the Cross in Kilmacolm, Renfrewshire with Pastors Ken and Bessie, and so it was to the river, which runs south of the village, that we made our way one Sunday afternoon. The weather was fine and the bees were busy collecting the pollen, when one of the young men was stung on the nose. It must have been very painful, but that did not stop the rest of the folk having a dig! Everywhere we went, an 'event' always happened, and we were glad when our turn was past. The Lord has a wonderful sense of humour especially when He chose us and loved us unconditionally! We were a motley crew, but the love felt among us was precious and rare.

One of the most momentous Baptismal Services was held in the lagoon at the then Hospitality Inn, Irvine, in 1995. Ten candidates came forward for immersion with sixty plus of an audience followed by lunch in the bistro area. Great excitement was in the air as we assembled as a Fellowship to hold our morning service with guitars, accordion, tambourines and singers. The praise resounded between the green decorative palm trees and tables, high up into the glass-domed ceiling. Unity and love was abroad that day as we sang 'Amazing Grace', it being the popular song of the day.

As the candidates were being baptised, the manager and his staff came around to see what it was all about, even the cleaners were leaning out of the apartment windows with dusters in hand to look on this amazing sight. What a witness and a privilege to testify of Jesus' saving grace and example of humility. After the original ten were baptised, an invitation was given to anyone else who desired to go through the waters of baptism, and who had Christ in their heart as Saviour, to come forward. One man came forward. Of course, we always had a spare shirt and trousers, 'just in case' there was an extra candidate, or two. What a morning! Only eternity will tell what transpired that day in the hearts and lives of those gathered.

These are the things that make the ministry worthwhile, that give joy and pleasure, and a deep knowing that He is leading every step of the way.

*The early days*

In the formative years of the Emmanuel Christian Centre, while we were both working in our respective secular jobs, we were full of enthusiasm to promote the Gospel of the Kingdom, and faith knew no bounds. The world was our oyster.

In the summers of 1985 and 1986, some of the highlights were when, by sheer unadulterated bravado, we hired the Volunteer Rooms in the town for a four-night campaign and invited Rev. Peter Scothern and Team to come and minister. It seemed ludicrously impossible, but we prayed and felt that it was right. Local churches were contacted, many leaflets were distributed and faith was high. Local newspapers got wind of what was about to happen in the Town and gave a good write-up and advertised nicely on our behalf. Brother Peter wrote to say he would be delighted to come to Irvine with ten of his team to minister and pray for the sick. We opened up our homes to the visitors and had sweet fellowship.

It was during this time that we applied to the New Testament Fellowship International, of which Rev Peter Scothern is Director, to become affiliated, and were accepted. There are NTFI churches all over the world, and we are pleased to be part of this great work.

People came from far and near – some in a minibus from Falkirk Town Mission, with a goodly number of the congregation. During the second evening of the campaign, in the middle of the service, a lady shouted out, "I can hear! I can hear!" She was about 36 years-of-age, and had been deaf since she was six-months-old. Friends had brought her, and they all went home rejoicing in their colleague's new healing and renewed faith.

A good number came through in salvation, and many were touched by the power of the Lord at work in their lives. Irvine had never seen such a move of the Holy Spirit in years, and it was the talk of the town for many months to come. Ten years later, people were still referring to the 'Healing Campaign'.

We were impressed to arrange another Campaign on the island of Arran two years later, and hired halls in Brodick, Corrie, Machrie, Pirnmill, Lochranza, the various villages around the island. Great were the deliverances and revelations at that time. Bessie Marsh and niece Jean gave us wonderful hospitality, and we all entered into the spirit of the campaign with great anticipation.

From time to time, we organised 'weekends away' to the Sannox Centre on Arran and took 16-18 people with us. Walking up Glen Rosa and climbing were two favourite pastimes – everyone always came back exhausted but happy, having been scratched to bits by hidden bramble bushes, or bitten to distraction by the midges – dock leaves have great healing properties we soon discovered. Then there were the midnight walks along the beach by torchlight, followed by past-midnight feasts of toast and cocoa. Stories and bedtime tales were the highlight of the day, and no one could tell a story quite like Duncan with his down-to-earth Glasgow humour always slipping in to the tale sideways.

Every morning, we donned our ECC (Emmanuel Christian

Centre) sweatshirts (that were, to put it mildly, rather on the 'neat' side by the end of the week), and out we went, distributing tracts and spreading the good news of the gospel. An appendix could be written about the many escapades and encounters along the way. These truly were the days of fun, laughter, and precious fellowship.

Both Duncan and I always desired simply to be a servant and a handmaid of the Lord, and that we would not in any way fall short of our potential in God, but be two people who would inspire and provide a model for others to follow. Pioneers in the spiritual sense of the word – ones who would not abort before the birth, or fail along the road that the Spirit of God chose for us. We had a magnificent obsession to be winners! The text of Paul the Apostle springs to mind:

- Oh that I might know Him in the power of His Resurrection and in the fellowship of His sufferings (Philippians 3:10).

As the good Book says: "*Without a vision the people perish*"! I believe the Lord of new days and new revelations would have us always to look forward and plan and keep excitement abreast of the disconsolate times we live in. You can have as dull a Christian life as you want, or as powerful and dynamic as you envision. God's open door in your life will cause you to think differently and give birth to amazing adventures in God.

## *House for sale!*

Never let it be said that we did not have a sense of humour, or did not laugh at ourselves and have fun. One such instance comes to mind.

We came back from a summer holiday one year having left the keys with Billy and Joyce to check the house and water the plants. That was fine, no problem, or so we thought.

On our return, we unpacked the car, said hello to a few of the neighbours, who seemed to look at us warily, which we thought strange, and we were just settling down, when the telephone rang. “Have you seen the notice on the study room window yet?” “No, we are not long home, what notice?” “Oh, while you were away we thought that we’d sell your house for you!”

We ran out into the garden and looked up at the small study window. There to our consternation was a for sale sign, and across it in red letters, sold. We fell about laughing. No wonder the neighbours were looking at us rather peculiarly. They thought this was for real, and that we had not told them we were moving before we went on holiday. When we explained the pranks that Billy and Joyce get up to, they also enjoyed and appreciated the humour. One man three doors down the road said, “I like that. I’ll tell that joke in the bar tonight!”

*The day of the big brown fox*

Looking out of the bedroom window here in Aberdeenshire at the whiter-than-white snow on 28th December 2005, reminds me of another day when the snow fell thick and fast – in the busy little town of Barrhead in Renfrewshire.

Duncan had made the acquaintance of a local businessman, ‘Bud’ by name, who had the contract to put in the fire-escape staircase. He had been extremely helpful in different areas of the work. One icy-cold morning, the telephone rang and it was our friend Bud to say that there was a lot of wood in the yard, which needed clearing out, and we could have it – free of charge – but some of it needed de-nailing! Not to be deterred, Duncan and his faithful worker, Brian, trundled up to Barrhead, suitably attired for the inclement weather with leather gloves, hat and all, to begin to clear the yard and load up the twelve-year-old church van! Hands were almost numb and the work began in earnest to de-nail the spare wood. Later, I overheard someone comment that most people would have scrapped it! But to know good wood when you see it is a bonus, and when it is 'dressed' up on the big machines, it can look like new!

As the snow came flurrying down thick and fast, Duncan tells the story. "Out of the corner of my eye, I had the suspicion that I was being observed. I glanced up, and to my amazement saw a large brown fox sitting in the backseat of an old abandoned car, watching my every move with great interest. It was as if he had nothing else to do, and he continued to watch us work until the job was finished – several hours later. The van was loaded up, yet he still sat and watched intently at all the goings on, and only stirred as the keys were put in the ignition and the engine turned over! 'Goodbye Mr Fox', we said, 'thank you for being our guest today and sitting so intently and patiently as we worked in the cold'. He only made a move to go when we drove off for home".

We went back to the same place a number of times, but we never ever saw him again! Was he sent to encourage us and spur us on at that time, we will never know this side of heaven. On our return, we told the story and all who heard were quite amused by the fox that hid in the car to get out of the cold and beheld a sight never to be seen again!

The wood, which was there for the taking, is now beautifully dressed and in place in the Emmanuel Christian Centre, West Road church building. Few there are who know the stories and the miracles behind the walls, and under their feet.

> One must have the eye of an eagle,
> be as wise a serpent,
> but as harmless as a dove.

This was the motto that 'Big Chief ' Duncan adopted at all times when work was in progress. On certain days, four, five sometimes six men would climb into the church van (driven by Pastor Duncan, of course) and go off hunting for materials. This particular day, one of the men quipped, “I am your eagle’s eye today, Duncan”. “Good”, was the reply, “Because today, we go left, young man”.

Down by the local industrial estate, the ‘eagle’s eye’ spied a factory being pulled down. “Let’s see what’s happening here”, said Duncan. Out he climbed, and talked to the charge-hand, and found out that all the material was to be transferred to the main site at Shettleston. “However”, said the man, “You could telephone the Director and tell him that you need the material, and it need never leave Irvine”. Instead of phoning, Duncan came home, changed and was off to Shettleston within the hour.

It just so happened that early the same morning, someone had contacted us with the news that they were going to give a gift of £500 towards the renovation of the Emmanuel Christian Centre, and that same sum was posted through the letter box shortly after.

Armed with faith, joy and a song in his heart Pastor Duncan drove to Shettleston to bargain for the much-needed timber and the other materials. On arrival in Glasgow, he witnessed to the Director of the contracting company about the faithfulness and goodness of God and the amazing leadings of the Holy Spirit in all areas of need during the renovation of the old church building. After all, “*this is the Lord’s doing and it is marvellous in our eyes*” is our watchword.

After half an hour of witness, the Director said, “Surely God is with you. If you can give me £500, the timber and all that is there is yours. It need not leave Irvine and come to the yard here. I don’t know why I am giving it to you for such a cut-down price; it is worth more than three times that amount, but you have convinced me your God is real”. Handshakes all round, telephone call to Irvine and the £500 handed over! (In the economy of God, there was no more and no less money than necessary for the need of the moment!) Faith and action once again moved the hand of God, and the heart of a Glasgow businessman!

The next few days were spent off-loading timber by the ton. Orders had been given to the site director in Irvine to load and deliver all the material to the West Road church building free of charge! God once again in Divine control!

During all these years, we received great encouragement through words of scripture and confirmation through many dear saints of God that Almighty God was with us, and that He would never leave us or indeed forsake us.

It was not always easy. At times, the way was extremely difficult. People left, others got impatient, some did not always understand the way of faith and criticised the man of God and his ways. But, if God has given you a vision, or a dream, then to pay attention to peoples' whims, words and moods will cause your dream to wither and die. We had each other, and we worked hand-in-hand together, encouraging, building each other up in the most holy faith. At times, it was soul-destroying and almost overwhelming when even family members disapproved of the work of faith and expressed their views loud and clear. What had we to do? Listen to man, or to God?

These early days of rebuilding were also heart-rending at times, because it was an onerous, burdensome task and most daunting, with a small congregation, little or no sure finances, but faith in a big God, yet knowing without shadow of doubt that He had called us to establish an end-time, apostolic, multi-purpose Centre locally, so that a people who sat in darkness could see and experience something worth living for and to bring hope to the needy. We could not express adequately or explain in human terms the call we felt on our lives at this time. It was a purpose-driven call to establish a work of God for His eternal glory.

It was a great day when Morton and his team drove up in the Notrom electrical vans. We knew something was going to be done that day, apart from chatting about what was happening in North Ayrshire and the churches all around. A great contribution to the work was much appreciated at that time.

Ronnie, the mechanic, took responsibility for the old church mini -bus and working vans, which we had from time to time, and did a miraculous job on them. Sometimes, we wondered how they managed to pass the mot test. Surely, the angels were with us in those days. Whenever Ronnie heard the old van of the moment roar up the street, he would hide his face in his hands, and say, “Oh my, what is it this time?” With great humour and expertise, he always got it going again. Thanks, Ronnie.

*The Water Board and the big brown pipe*

No recordings would be complete without the following story. A representative from the local Water Board authority told us that in order to have mains water piped into the church, we would have to get permission for the road to be dug up across to the other side, where the main water pipe was located in order for a connection to be made to it. Not only that, we would also need to cone off the road and divert the traffic. All of this would cost us in excess of £1,000.

We were always very careful with the monies entrusted to us, and we both felt that there was something not quite right about this water project. So it was down to prayer and hearing from God who alone knows all things.

One day, Duncan said to me, “I just know there is a pipe at this side of the church (outside the front door), but all the maps of the area indicate that the pipe is on the other side, just as the man from the Water Board said. I am going to hire an electric digger tomorrow, and see what is down there”. True to his word, he and Brian started digging, and by three o’clock in the afternoon, they hit something hard. With their hands, they removed the gritty, damp, black earth surrounding the object. To their delight, they came across a large, round, brown water pipe!

Without hesitation, Duncan ran to the Water Board offices to tell them of his find. They told him that even going back two hundred years, there was no recorded mains pipe in that vicinity, but, as they were soon to close for the day, they would come in the morning to see what he had found.

Sure enough, there they were, first thing in the morning, to see this rare sight. However, it had to be tested with a blue dye to make doubly certain that the water ran out to the connecting mains pipes. A shout of "goodness gracious me" went up when it passed the test. The Water Board men just could not believe the tenacity of this man, who proved to one and all that there just had to be a better way out of this dilemma, and the cost was a mere fraction of the original. What a mighty God we serve! It pays to listen for the still small voice, for in it there is victory all the way. Word soon went round the members in the fellowship that God again had answered prayer in a most miraculous way. Songs of victory and triumph resounded!

## *Rolls, rolls and yet more rolls of carpeting*

It had been quiet a morning, catching up with the usual household chores after a busy weekend, when the telephone rang. "How are you getting on with the renovation work? Are you about ready to get the carpeting for the church?", asked Donnie at the other end of the telephone. "Well, it is like this, it will probably be a good year plus before we will be in a position to think about carpeting. It is a big place, and there are other things to attend to before we consider the floor covering".

The next part of the conversation went like this: "We have had a consignment of carpeting returned to our company because the colour is not quite the shade the customer had ordered and as the

Big brown water pipe

The Scaling arrives

company is folding up, we need to get rid of it, there is enough to do your church, can you come and see it?"

Hurriedly, I drove down to West Road to tell Duncan all about the carpet conversation. "We'll go right away, and strike while the iron is hot". Quick wash and change then over to Kilmarnock for viewing.

We could not believe our eyes when we saw this beautiful carpeting rolled out on the tarmac yard. It had a lovely neutral background with a touch of green relief on five rolls, and a touch of terracotta on the other five. This was a lot of carpeting but we had big spaces to cover from downstairs in the multi-purpose area, to upstairs in the sanctuary, as well as the wide sweeping staircase. "This looks absolutely amazing", was our response. "How much would it cost?" Not to worry about a thing. It would be delivered to the Emmanuel Christian Centre free of charge, and the percentage cost would be taken care of. Just be blessed!

Blessings like this could only be arranged in heaven – this was a miracle of the God-kind. No wonder the saints could hardly contain themselves – it was mind-blowing. When the time came to lay the carpets, we would not be thinking about what colour would be best, where to buy, what quality? It was all taken care of by a bountiful Father. The people who come after us must know and hear about the miracles that God performed on our behalf. He is just the same today and tomorrow. He does not change when your trust is in Him.

## *I will speak, if you will listen*

"The Lord spoke to me in the night Greta, saying to go to Millport on the island of Cumbrae (about an hour's journey), climb the high hill, and He would have a word for me". As I had other things to attend to that day, I said that we could talk when we were home in the evening.

It was late when Duncan came home, brimming with happiness and a feeling of well-being. There is nothing like being obedient to the voice of the Lord of Lords. To get to the high hill on Cumbrae is quite a walk uphill, but on a good day, the view is quite spectacular. While Duncan was admiring the view, who should appear over the hill but Pastor John Carr from Dundee! Simultaneously, they asked each other what they were doing up on the hill! As both servants of God were led by the Spirit of God, they knew that it was a Divine appointment. They sat, drew on the Word of God and prayed. Then an answer came in a word of knowledge through brother John to Duncan, which set his mind at rest for the next part of the journey. Our God is everywhere, and He will never leave us or forsake us.

We both thanked God for His word of encouragement, which spurred us on to the next level of faith.

*Fire escape staircase*

This was to be a massive undertaking and an expensive one. We did not know where to begin. So it was down to real praying, hearing from God, sending for estimates, having the contractors in to measure up etc. By this time, we were used to people coming in with their ideas and clipboards.

All the estimates were away beyond our budget; they all seemed so prohibitive. Weeks passed and this big undertaking was always on the back of our mind. Coming back to Irvine from Barrhead one day, along a road that we did not normally use, Duncan put his foot on the brake and signalled to pull in. Was that a wrought iron workshop?

Do they make fire escapes? Yes! They made fire escapes to plan, and indeed, they would come and give us a reasonable estimate.

We had been given estimates of up to £15,000 for a fire escape. It pays to look around, and especially pray, for the right person to do the right job. The men came, measured up, and the estimate was under £4,000! Now we felt a release to ask Heaven for help to clear this bill. And He did! Let me say here, that we never borrowed a single pound, neither did we ever consider lottery money. When we had a bill to pay, we interceded, and trusted God alone. God moved the hearts of the 'whosoever' on hearing of the project to plant a seed into the work of the Emmanuel Christian Centre, and were blessed themselves by doing this.

The men worked really well and did an excellent job. When it was finished, friends painted it from top to bottom and it looked as good as any contractor could have done. God gives the best when the choice is left to him. Duncan and the boss of the firm became good friends and helped each other, Duncan often witnessed to him concerning the miracles that the Lord had performed on our behalf. To God be all the glory.

Some, who have never known the nights of prayer, the agonising over contracts, wondering where all the finances were going to come from, run up and down this same staircase without a thought of what it took to get it in place. Only God knows, as well as the team members and interested friends, of the years of petitioning the Holy Spirit to answer prayer. But oh the joy when the answers came! Nothing, simply nothing, can compare to the thrill in one's heart and spirit when you know that you know that you have really been in touch with Heaven, and that the God of all grace has made a way where there seemed to have been no way!

What worship resulted from these miracles; we would not have had it any other way. We, in the Emmanuel Christian Centre, have been so privileged to be chosen by God to experience His dealings, and to get to know His voice, and His way, in these days of worldly compromise. Thank you Lord.

## *There is coming a day of happy reunion*

In the ensuing years, I do not know where Duncan finished and I began. Our lives were intertwined and heaven-propelled. Our immediate family, Gillies and Elaine, never questioned the call of God on our lives, as they understood from early childhood that God was pre-eminent in all things, and they were loved and very special. Our little son, and their brother, Duncan Max is in heaven waiting our reunion. What a day that will be!

From the earliest years, we four sang – mainly in the car on the way back from a meeting – prayed and laughed together and talked of the great Salvation that Jesus wrought for mankind on the Cross of Calvary. The Word says, "*Bring up a child in the way he should go, and when he is old he will not depart from it*". Children are so precious and a gift from God.

Our son Gillies is married to Celia, and they have two boys, Ross and Jack, who live in Aberdeenshire. Elaine is married to Brian and they live in Yorkshire. My nearest relatives are Duncan's brother Robin and his wife Sandra, daughters Tanya and Lara, who live in Glasgow. My brother and his wife live up the west coast. Our family used to be very big when we attended weddings, etc. but in the last ten years has dwindled dramatically. I guess it is the process of growing older!

## *Church windows*

On a dull, grey, Monday morning, the old front door of the church opened and a well-known voice shouted, "Are you there Duncan? How is the project going; been thinking about you. Have you ordered the high windows yet?"

Well, that was a big item, and no, we had not ordered the windows, far less even thought that far ahead.

The voice was that of an old-time friend who was the manager for a well-known double-glazing firm, and was ready to help us in this matter.

Without further ado, out came the measuring tapes, and the boarded-up windows were measured for height and width. Seventeen feet high! How much would that cost? This was quickly followed by a barrage of other questions. Then, by faith, we placed the order, and sought the Lord concerning the price.

The afternoon arrived when a few 'friends' and their truck trundled up to Glasgow for the very large windows. The wind was a howling gale, and so the glass windows were tied between mattresses to keep them from cracking on the return journey. What a relief when at last the truck came round the corner of West Road with every window intact – eight very large windows in all, to be exact. We all shouted "Hallelujah"!

But what about the price, and where did the money come from? We knew that this would be one of the most expensive items that we would ever have to buy in the renovation of the old church. Previously, we had been given an estimate for the windows, and this figure was way above £18,000!

One of the mottos we held on to was – "I will, if you will. If you show me your faith in action, I will act on your faith". We set about real prayer, crushing more cans, bringing in old jewellery to sell, unwanted books, etc.

Our old-time friend wanted to bless us, but the price had to go through the company's books and so we had to be honourable and pay our share. Soon, the morning came when an official letter plopped through the letter box at 2 West Road with the bill for the beautiful, snow-flake arch top design seventeen-feet tall windows. Duncan went pale, and I asked him, "How much?" "If the figures had been reversed, it would be all right, as we have that in the kitty, but this is four times more than what we have!"

We did not see our friend for the next two weeks, but all the time, we were storming heaven for more monies to come in, but they never did. When our friend did appear, and saw the windows stacked up, he asked whether we were satisfied with everything. "How do you get out of this one?", Duncan thought?

"Everything would have been all right had the figures been reversed", said the bold man. To our amazement, our gracious friend said, "No problem! What do you have? I'll alter it right now and call it a done deal!" We had had two weeks of sleepless nights, wondering how it would all pan out, and all the time God had it in hand. Sometimes, He just does not let you know. Will we ever learn to trust Him fully in all things at all times?

Today, we do not give it another thought, and I am sure that the people who walk in and out of the building in years to come will never know how some had to walk the walk of faith. That is why this book has been written and made available in order to encourage others who are embarking on a similar walk.

*Appointment in the Supermarket*

"What are you doing here at this time of the morning, shouldn't you be working in our church building getting it ready?" So challenged one old dear as she came into the Asda store for her groceries on a Monday morning in the late Spring of 1995.

Once again Duncan had heard from the Lord, and the story goes like this: "I have prepared my servant's heart to help finance the next phase of the project and he will meet you in the new supermarket with my abundance"!

In obedience Duncan went and had a coffee and sat towards the entrance to the supermarket tearoom where he could see everyone coming through the revolving door.

He waited and waited, and no one came. So it was back to the grind still trusting God.

Tuesday came and went and still no one came. On the Wednesday, the same old dear appeared through the doors of the supermarket again to see her Pastor drinking more coffee as if he had nothing else to do. She moved on, talking away to herself and shaking her head (so would you or I if we had witnessed this scene). He was just about to leave after his second cup of coffee and a bit disillusioned wondering if he really had picked up God rightly, when a smiling FGBMFI brother came sweeping through the doors of the supermarket!

"Oh, I've been meaning to come and see you for a few days now Duncan. The Lord told me to give you this", and pulled a handsome cheque out of his inside pocket.

That morning. his wife had wanted to do her shopping in Irvine, and so the divine appointment came to pass.

On the Sunday morning, Duncan was free to tell all (including the dear old lady) that this had been the will of God and you have to persist and pursue sometimes just like Daniel. The angel had heard his prayer the first time, but it took some time to battle through the principalities and powers.

There were great shouts of "victory", when the congregation heard we had another few thousand pounds to continue with the on-going project.

An important lesson can be learned from this event:

*Do not ask the Lord to guide your footsteps if you are not willing to move your feet.*

*"Country lanes, not the usual motorways"*

One Sunday morning, sister Jeanette said that she had had a

dream from the Lord regarding the work of the Emmanuel Christian Centre. "The Lord showed me that the Centre is like a bus, which will not take the usual route of the other buses, but will take the country lanes and go along the highways and byways. Some will get on at the beginning and stay to the end, others will get on and get off the bus perhaps halfway through the journey; others will yet again alight the bus, as it meanders through the lanes letting off and picking up the people until the terminus is reached. This bus will take the unusual routes, not the straight motorway, because it is His peculiar work".

## *Don't count your chickens until they are hatched*

The servant of the Lord who stencilled out the lettering for the wall poster, Gil, has now gone to his reward in Heaven, having laboured diligently in the service of His Master. Duncan had a saying that he had learned from his Principal at Bible School, his beloved Pastor Ian Macpherson – God buries his workmen, but His work goes on! We have had to learn the awful reality of that statement in recent years both as a Fellowship and personally.

We all talked constantly and witnessed tirelessly of the miracles that God had performed on our behalf. There was always an excitement in the air of what the Lord was about to do next. One day, early into the renovation work, we had a telephone call from a Team Member, "Money, in the form of a large cheque, was to be given to us to help complete the project". The person wanted to remain anonymous. The cheque was duly handed over; we sat outside the church building and gave thanks to God for such a large sum, enough to see the project completed.

Because a law had been passed one year before, only the person, or the Company, whose name was written on the cheque could lodge it in their account. We had to contact the person to have it paid into their account and subsequently into the Emmanuel Christian Centre's Bank Account. In the process of this happening, the person concerned changed their mind and our hopes and plans were dashed to pieces! During previous conversations, we had said, on more than one occasion to the person, "Do you really want to give us such a large sum?" "Oh yes. I've promised this for the work of the Lord; I don't need it, and anyway, I don't want to be an Ananias or a Sapphira!" Only God knows the hearts of all people. However, after the shock wave passed, we felt, "Well Lord, it was lovely to dream!" Thank God, we had not arranged for contractors to come in on the strength of that vow! If we had done so, we would have been in severe debt and so ashamed at running ahead of God. As the old adage says – Don't count your chickens until they are hatched.

"Shall we tell the congregation?" the informed member asked. Together we said "No". It is always better to be safe than sorry. We were so glad that we never declared the cheque at that time. Although we were cautious and thanked God for His great provision, when the blow fell, honestly speaking, we were devastated. I telephoned a sister-in-the-Lord, a confidante, at that time; she took it before the Lord and carried our burden through until we got the victory over the disappointment. It was not until four months later that Pastor Duncan mentioned in the morning sermon that we had had a cheque in our hand for £77,815.00 (an awful lot of money in 1993). However, "*The Lord giveth and the Lord also taketh away*"! Nobody seemed too upset, but it was a hard test of faith for us both, as it could have made the work a lot easier and hastened the day of completion, but it was not to be.

As in all great works of God, "*unless you are tried, you cannot come forth as gold*" (Job 23:10). From that time on, we picked ourselves up, dusted ourselves down, and got on with God's good work, having the backing of His Word and His eternal love.

God always gives light relief in times of hard trials. We looked forward every summer to a break when we could pack the car and drive off into the sunset – to network, meet old friends, and make new friends, visit places and of course, fit in a conference or two!

In the course of two decades, from 1982 until 2002, we enjoyed travelling to conferences in the summer, the outstanding ones being Colin Urquhart's Faith Camp in Peterborough to which our friend Enid introduced us. Then there was Ken Gott's church in Sunderland, Michael Bassett's church, London, Vicki Jamieson-Peterson's ministry, Pastor Don & Heather Double's Camp Meetings in Malvern, Mahev Chavda's ministry, Sharon Stone's Ministry in the Round House, and Loughborough, Paul Scanlon and Abundant Life Church, Bradford, and Hollybush Camp in Northallerton. In the winter months, we liked to network and support the local conferences in Scotland and further afield whenever time permitted.

*Appointment with Oral Roberts as praying-partners*

One outstanding Divine appointment comes to mind. We were thrilled to receive an invitation from the great healing evangelist Oral Robert to attend a Day Conference at a Manchester hotel, as we were prayer partners and supported the ministry. We were so excited at being invited; it was like a dream come true. As we were going into the hotel, Duncan helped a man up a few stairs since he appeared to have great difficulty in walking. We took our place at one of the long tables at which lunch would be served after the morning meeting. Oral spoke on the blessings of giving and receiving just as the harvest follows the sowing of the seed. Towards the end of the convocation, Oral came round the tables, laid hands on each individual and prayed for them. There were about two hundred present that day. What joy and peace filled our beings; we were blessed beyond measure!

That day was a never to be forgotten event in our lives. Going back downstairs that evening, the gentleman we had met on the way in, leapt down the stairs with a grin the size of a Cheshire cat, shouting praises to the Lord all the way! Then it was back home with precious, treasured memories stored in our hearts.

Perceton Country Church

1994—May 2004

Upstairs Sanctuary

Emmanuel Christian Centre, 2 West Road, Irvine

Multi-Purpose area

## *Perceton country church*

By the year 1994, we had worshipped in three different venues since buying the old church, and we were now in the Congregational Church hall, Dreghorn. The time came again, when we knew that it was time to move on. That feeling was confirmed when the elders wanted to put up the rent from £40 per month to £40 per week! It was time to move on.

Thursday was our day off, so we set out to look for a suitable venue early one morning. We searched all day with no joy, but coming home by way of Perceton House, I happened to look round as we were about to cross the river bridge, and saw what looked like a little mission hall perched on a hill. I said to Duncan, "If you can, would you reverse, and we can have a look at what appears to be a little church". Although the darkness was beginning to descend by this time, we backtracked and parked beside a clump of trees. On ascending the small hill, we discovered the building to be of fair size, with boarded up windows on both sides. Bushes covered what once might have been a path round the old hall. We felt a peace about it and set about enquiring who owned it. After two or three months, we tracked down the person who held the key along with the trustees responsible for the building.

After we had gone around the building, inside and out, we decided that with a good coat of paint, the windows repaired and carpeting laid, we could camp there quite comfortably for a peppercorn rent, until the church at West Road was ready. A makeshift toilet was installed before a proper one could be set in place in the old vestry. What fun and games we had that first year, as it was very cold. Everybody was really brave, but most of us had a good sense of humour, which came in handy, especially as the kitchen had little visitors who would eat any crumbs left about. The spiders saw to the rest. Eddie and Cathie who live in the house across the road were very kind to us and helped out many a time. Eddie, being a bit of an artist, painted a baptismal scene on the far wall, which everyone admired as it depicted Duncan baptising a young boy in the river, and on either side were tall Canadian fir trees with a village high up in the mountains!

One story comes to mind, which Duncan loved to tell. It happened in the early years in Perceton church, around 1996. Frank, the plumber, wanted a pipe to run from the kitchen to the vestry, which was a good thirty feet in length, to enable the water to flow from one area to another, across the outside path, down the hillside, under the car park and into the river! There was only one problem, the space under the floorboards, along which the water pipe had to run, was only eight inches deep. Duncan had sawn out a square at either end – the problem was to get the pipe from one end to another. One of the 'Job Creation' boys thought it would be a good idea to go across the road for Eddie's little dog, put him in at one end, tie the pipe to its leg, have a sausage at the other end and entice it to run underneath the floorboards from one end to the other, pulling the pipe behind it.

When Duncan arrived back with the dog and sausage, the job had been done! What miracle had taken place? When the Pastor was away, Mick volunteered to crawl underneath the floor explaining that it was his hobby to undertake such jobs, as he was thin, wiry and knew exactly what to do, as his profession had been breaking into places in the dead of night! The tale was told by everyone for a very long time to come. The 'Job Creation' men laid paths round the Hall, built a BBQ, and a Jacob's well among other things. We bought chips for the car park to give it some foundation, and built a fence round the perimeter to keep the children from slipping into the river.

Years previously, at the very beginning of the work, we were invited by Rudolph and May Dehn to go with them to a counselling week in a priory in Ditchingham, led by Bill and Molly Warboys. After a few days of real soul searching at the

Conference, we were asked to see the leaders in the back room – we wondered what we had done! Molly had had a dream in the night and wanted to share it with us. In the dream, she saw a large field, a river with trees on both sides, and caravans nearby, the Lord impressed in her spirit that we would worship in a place surrounded by such, but it would not be the hub, but a spoke from the hub. One day, years later, Duncan and I were leaning over the railings at Perceton Mission Hall taking in the view, when suddenly this dream that Molly had all those years ago came flooding back to my mind, and I said to Duncan – "Remember Molly Warboys and the dream she had, there it is all before us: the river, the trees, the large field, and the caravans, and this is not our final resting place, it is West Road church!" Surely, the vision will be completed, and it was in His time and in His way. The Lord be praised.

For some unknown reason, the prayer meetings were well attended by men and women. I can only think back on reflection that it was because we had a goal to meet and we had on the wall a challenge for all to see: the vision will be completed. We had to pray in all the workers, the materials, the finance, keep the church mini-bus on the road such as it was, and Duncan and I had a peppercorn salary. Glory to God, I do not know how we managed, but we did! Even when people left, the vision carried on because He is God and His will shall not be thwarted! It was miracle after miracle and we would not have had it any other way. We were enjoying the journey.

Speakers came from the north of Scotland to the borders, from Estonia and America There are a few who stand out, namely Barbara from Kilsyth who ministers in the prophetic quite profoundly. The 'little church on the prairie', as we used to call it, had never seen such spiritual might in its life. Many a time, we ambled down the hill to our cars singing the praises of the Most High God, hearts ready to burst at the goodness of God towards His people. Nothing, simply nothing can compare to the anointing of the Lord when the Holy Spirit is present among His people to bless.

*Building up dividing walls*

We had unfinished dividing walls in the multi-purpose areas, but prices were escalating and time was short. We needed a miracle to complete the job before the electricians descended on us in two weeks' time.

The morning was bright and sunny at 8 o'clock one Tuesday morning in May, as off the willing volunteers went in the church van, over hill and dale, not taking the usual route. Cutting across unknown area of land, they happened to stumble upon a quarry. Before their eyes, they spied the exact blonde stone they were looking for! It was now mid-day, the men were hungry but there was more important business to attend to.

Duncan went straight into the site office where he was informed that all the stone was going back to Penrith in a few days' time, because it was old stock. "Is it for sale?" "No" came the stark reply. Question, "Why don't we take it off your hands, and save you shipment costs?" Reply, "Come back in a few days time, and we'll let you know what Head Office says, as some of the stones are imperfect at the corners and have to be segregated".

On the way back to Irvine, there was an air of expectancy and rejoicing, as there was no doubt in anyone's mind this was the leading of the Lord.

When the Intercessors' Group heard of this latest adventure in faith, we all just praised and thanked the Lord. The stones, which were sorely needed, were being made available to us at reduced cost!

God is ever faithful. On arriving back at the quarry towards the end of the week, the first stop was again the office to hear the decision from Head Office. "You can have all the stone you require, and instead of it being £2.22 per stone, because some of them are chipped, you can have them for the taking away for 22p each. Take as many as you require!"

This was indeed a miracle of the God kind.

The stones were piled high, and, as the men were looking for the best, somehow Duncan's hand got caught in between the stones. Some were dislodged, and a mountain of stone came crashing down on his left hand. He thought that his fingers at least would be crushed, if not broken. The men gathered round and eased his wrist and hand out of the heap of stone, which now lay everywhere like an avalanche. For this job, the men had been equipped with hard hats and thick, leather, working gloves. Duncan told me afterwards that when he eased off the glove, he fully expected his fingers to be in pieces so great was the pain; and he also said that at moment of impact, he had shouted the name of "Jesus" for all in the yard to hear. His fingers were very badly bruised, but not a bone was broken, praise the Name of the Lord. This did not deter the pioneer; he soldiered on until all the stone required was safely deposited in West Road. The walls were built up in record time, praise be to the God who never fails.

Days of economic crisis will come, but our God, Emmanuel, has an abundant supply of whatever we need, we just have to listen for the still soft voice of the Holy Spirit saying, "This is the way, walk in it". The motto of this miracle-story is, "When you know without doubt God that is leading you, persist and pursue until the answer that you require comes and leads you into praise and victory".

*Short visit to keswick*

I sought the Lord greatly as we went to Keswick for a few days that year. The name 'cameo' had come to me a few times – Come And Meet Each Other – especially Jesus, who else in this troubled world with all its stress and pressures?

I was rummaging in a box marked 'everything £1', when I heard these ladies say, "Oh this and this will do for our Ladies Cameo!" I could not contain my interest, and enquired about their 'Cameo'. One of them said, "We have named our ladies' ministry, cameo, come and meet each other!" Well, that was enough confirmation for me, so when I returned home I shared the God appointment with the members, and we have continued to meet ever since on the third Thursday of every month. Speakers come and share what God has done for them, but more than that, the ladies grow in God and in the power of His might. Most certainly a time of encouragement and real blessing.

Quite a number of the ladies used to come from Troon, a town four miles away, so we set up a satellite cameo for them on the first Thursday of the month in the South Beach Hotel. A number of other women have joined the group led by Wendy, Ann and Margaret, which is proving profitable. It is always a joy and a time of relaxation to pop in and enjoy the fellowship of the women.

Breakthrough Weekends are arranged with special speakers once a year at a Christian location for reflection and ministry and excellent fellowship.

*The secret cottage in the country*

There were times when the way got tough, or things were not working out as we had hoped and we had to battle through in faith. The enemy of our souls had plans for us to lose heart, give up and fail. There were delays and denials for a period of two years at the start of the new millennium. During these difficult days, we had to seek solitude in order to spend more time in prayer and in the Bible. We would go for long walks, sing praises to the Lord in the countryside and listen for His voice in the stillness of the day or night.

Our faithful friend, Bessie, from Brodick on the Isle of Arran had passed on to her reward. We had few other places to which we could safely withdraw for peace and quiet in order to reflect and plan for the future, so we took this matter to the Lord in prayer.

Down in the Borders of Scotland there are many delightful, original stone-built cottages tucked away in secluded woodland with walks and brooks and wild flowers in abundance. A place to make one's heart leap and be lifted out of the sombre and sometimes conflicting issues of life. We know without a shadow of doubt that during the last few years of Duncan's life, we were Divinely led to enquire if a certain cottage was available for a few days, as it was imperative that we 'come apart and be still'. As people with a God-project know, there are many enemies and the usurper would hinder at every turn and thwart God's will if at all possible. At that time, we did not know of course that the Lord had plans to take Duncan home in November 2003.

The first time we went to the Galloway coast, we did not know the area, so the owner of the cottage kindly came to meet us in his car, and we followed him along the unfamiliar terrain. When we finally swept up the driveway and turned the corner, there, in front of us, was the cottage of our dreams! We had arrived to find a little bit of heaven here on earth. This lovely Irish family made us so very welcome with fresh eggs from the hens that strutted about the enclosed garden, milk and bread. We were so happy and could hardly contain our joy. The question is often asked, "Where were you when the twin towers were blown apart?" That day we had decided not to watch any television until 10 p.m. I was upstairs reading, oblivious to what half the world knew, when Duncan shouted upstairs, "Greta! You had better come down and see the news, something dreadful has happened in America"! We sat and watched as the awful drama unfolded. It reminded me of God's word "*everything that can be shaken will be shaken*". Thirty years ago, Morris Cerullo, a powerful prophetic preacher, received that very word. It is now happening rapidly all over the earth.

Even on the dullest day, our secret cottage was a haven of rest and tranquillity. We soon got to know the best places for homemade soup and coffee, and of course, never tired of speaking to the people we met of the wonderful works of God and the miracles He performed on our behalf. One Wednesday afternoon, on a woodland walk, Duncan told me that he was tired of jumping up and down onto a chair to measure the doorposts and lintels in the church building, and could we pray that a young man whom he had seen in our local shopping mall would come to the Centre and help. This young man was very tall, well over 6ft 6ins in height, whereas Duncan was 5ft 9ins. If he worked for us, he could just reach up and give the measurement without jumping on and off a chair.

Back home, we saw the man in the street and told the Lord that he was the one needed for the work ("*a willing volunteer in the day of His power*" (Psalm 110:3)). At that time, we did not know that he was unemployed and looking for something to do during the day. Two weeks later, in walked that young man, Colin, by name and said, "I've been sent here by the Job Centre, as I've joined the 'Job Creation' scheme, and wondered if you could take me on?" Duncan had him working and measuring up within the hour! God hears and answers prayer, hallelujah! In the services that weekend, there was great rejoicing. He was a good worker and a very likeable lad. Eventually, after six months, the young man left, and God blessed him with a good job in the Civil Service.

## *The first women's work and ministry*

This work is close to my heart as from a young married wife and mother, I presided and organised gatherings for the women of the church and loved the fellowship, teaching and companionship that this brought.

Having left the Pentecostal fellowship under God's direction, practically all I had ever known in my life, I ventured out in faith again and sought to raise up a women's work. Quite a number of ladies, who had joined with us at the beginning, when we worshipped in the building at 152 High Street, were enthusiastic, so we began in the winter of 1983 with local speakers, home-brew praisers, egg sandwiches and homemade scones. Many were the blessings in those bygone days. We saw women saved, baptised in the Holy Spirit, yet others were healed. There was real blessing in the gatherings as we prayed and waited on the Lord. Friends from Manchester told me of a new women's movement which had started in England called 'Women's Aglow Fellowship', and that the people involved were really enthusiastic and on fire for God.

Through a series of events, I met a few of the ladies who had been instrumental in establishing this work in England, namely Mary Hailes, Margaret Bell and Winifred Ascroft. I attended a meeting with a friend and enjoyed it immensely; I liked what I saw and heard. Not long afterwards, we discovered that an 'Aglow' meeting had begun in Scotland, in the Esquire House Hotel, Glasgow, with Loanne Duvall, Anita and Allyson being on the first local Board. From then on, once a month, four or five of us would pack into a car and travel 25 miles to the 'Aglow'. It was 1984. Oh the glory of the praise, testimonies and excitement of the fellowship. We saw signs and wonders, and made firm friendships that have lasted to this day.

Two years later, we also of the Emmanuel Christian Centre became affiliated to 'Women's Aglow Fellowship' as it was known then, and attended the annual Conferences in Southport. They were first held in the Prince of Wales Hotel, and later in the Floral Hall. There was such singing and dancing in the Spirit when the Glory of God fell on the gatherings; anointed women from all over the world attended, and went back to their nation blessed. We wore our new 'WAF' badge with pride. Many new friends were made over the years, which is all part of God's great plan of networking His people together.

Eventually, we had to move the monthly meeting out to a neutral venue – the local Stanecastle Hotel, where we saw many lives changed in the name of God's Son, Jesus the Deliverer. 'Aglow' is still alive and well twenty-plus years later with a good number of Chapters now in Scotland.

As God always does, He makes you restless in your spirit when He wants you to move on, deeper into Him and higher to another level, into that place of abiding in Him.

*Atlanta, Georgia, USA*

One day I said to the Lord in a whispered prayer, "Lord, it would be lovely if someone organised a conference/holiday for me as I am always the one to do the organising. I would like a nice surprise. You choose". Sometimes, God works in a hurry and this was one of these times. The telephone rang a few days later, and the voice at the other end said, "We are planning to go to a conference and there are three of us wanting to go, but we need another person to make up the four; so we thought of you. Would you like to join us?" Would I not! Arrangements all made for me, wow! When I asked where it was being held (thinking it would be somewhere in Britain), I was told that it was in Atlanta, Georgia, USA! I had never been to America, and I thought, "Well God, you don't do things by half, you make it big".

The great day came when Barbara, Joyce and I boarded the plane, and off we went to the End-Time Handmaidens Conference in the deluxe Westin Peachtree Plaza Hotel. Barbara's friend Linda was meeting us in America. We arrived on Saturday 29th July 2000 into opulence of the Dallas kind – wall-lined mirrors, marble pillars and floors, doors and lifts going everywhere. The whole place buzzing with people of many nationalities and colours. This was America as never seen before.

Speakers included Gwen Shaw, Founder and President of End-time Handmaidens and Servants, Arthur Burt, a contemporary of Smith Wigglesworth, Robert Shattles, Pastor of a church in Austell, Georgia, a man overflowing with the Holy Spirit and His Glory. We evidenced the gold dust and oil from heaven as he ministered. Pete Snyder, missionary-adventurer in both Haiti and China. As the week progressed, angels were seen to be present in the meetings!

Three things stand out in my mind, which really blessed us was first, the grand piano musical renderings, then the violins playing, and finally the beautiful singing voice of Sharon Buss. We learned how to use the 'flag ministry' to great advantage when interceding and fasting. Months of preparation went into the making of a gold replica of the Ark of the Covenant, also crowns on red, green and blue velvet cushions depicting Jesus Christ as both King and Priest. Beautifully mounted banners illustrating the four beasts of the book of Revelation were on display throughout the week.

On my return from the conference, there was a great stirring in my spirit to enter into the End-Time Handmaidens' twenty-one day fast, to seek His face for a deepening of spiritual life with Jesus my Lord and Saviour. That journey opened my eyes to see the areas in my life that needed attention – corners in the rooms of my heart that needed to be swept clean, unforgiveness that had to be addressed. Years later, (May 2006) while holidaying in Israel, I took the vow of an End-Time Handmaiden in the House of Peace in Jerusalem. That was a solemn moment to remember for the rest of my life.

*The word says: "offences will come"*

Up until that particular time, I had held on to an offence and was not prepared to let it go – until towards the end of the fasting. (Oh, how that gets rid of the rubbish in one's heart!)

I was in prayer one day, when before my eyes as in a dream, I looked in on a living room scene in a friend's house, and to my amazement, I saw people who had caused us great pain.

"What does this mean Lord?" I asked.

In the middle of the fast, I had cried to the Lord to heal me of all the wounds and hurts of bygone years, but I did not know the answer would come in vision form. I had put my fleece out to the Lord and said, "Lord, will you make a way for me to make peace, I can't, but you can, you arrange it". At this point, I heard a small whisper, "I'll tell you where to go, and you will love those people as though nothing had ever happened to upset you". My thoughts at that point were, "This is really a big thing, God".

Three weeks later, on the way back to my car having been to the local supermarket, the Lord dropped the bombshell. "This is the day that I have arranged for you to meet in a mutual friend's house, and you will tell the people you love them". My first reaction was, "Not today Lord, I need to get home, unpack the shopping, and begin to prepare the evening meal; then get ready for the evening service". All was silent. The Holy Ghost has a way of making you feel mean when you rebel against His will. After a great struggle, I surrendered. The Lord reminded me that I had asked Him to cleanse me afresh. He took me at my word, arranged a time for this to be put right, and here I was questioning, debating, wanting to opt out of His appointment.

With great trepidation, I drove to the address, not knowing what to expect, trying to sing on the way, but nothing gelled, only the scene before my eyes. On arrival, I observed there was no car in the car park, so perhaps I had mistaken the leading of the Lord after all, and began to feel a bit brighter. Anyhow, I would visit my friend and come away quickly. As I rang the doorbell, I just knew that the Lord was with me. I sensed the Holy Spirit's enabling power coming upon me. "How lovely to see you", was the warm welcome as the door opened, "But there are some people in today". No turning back now, it had to be a going forward in the Name of the Lord.

Just as in the picture, there were the people sitting around the room. Whenever eyes met, there was a melting and a fusing of Calvary love, tears flowed and a great battle was won that day. The drive home was one of high-sounding praises to the Champion of Champions! Oh the joy of just knowing that you have been obedient to the will of the Father, and oh the Glory of His Presence when the pure knowledge dawns that there is nothing between; the Presence of the Holy Spirit is so sweet.

Later that evening, when I told Duncan about the way the Lord had led me that day, he also had an exciting drama to unfold, and together, we marvelled at the goodness of the Lord in the land of the living. If we want to be great in God's Kingdom, we must learn to be a servant of all.

### *Unexpected sources*

One morning, we had a visit from the local MP Brian Donoghue, and as he bounded upstairs in the now half-renovated building to see how the project was coming along, he posed the question, "I don't suppose you would be interested in lottery money?" We both replied simultaneously, "No", and his next comment was that he did not think we would. We proceeded to tell him the reason why, which is found in the scriptures from Proverbs 22:7 "*The rich rule over the poor, and the borrower is a servant to the lender*".

We put our trust in God to build His church with clean money from the very outset, and He would continue to do so. However, Mr Donoghue said that he had a good friend in Richard Branson, who also owed him a favour. Later, when Mr Donoghue related to him what we were doing and what stage the project was at, we received a sizeable cheque, which helped us complete the next part of the work.

Two representatives from the Virgin Corporation flew to Scotland, came to Irvine, and presented us with the cheque. As they were viewing upstairs, Mr Branson's PA, a beautiful black lady, started to sing a gospel chorus, which really blessed our hearts and made our day. It was times like this that made the sacrifice of the work worthwhile and brought a lot of joy and happiness to the Team Members and other workers who came along to help.

*Poems and encouragements*

***To Pastor Greta by Ann***

Whatever the task, be it great or small
You give your everything, you give your all.
Closely you walk by the side of the Master
Your faith's so strong, not once do you falter.
Your love and compassion is surely God-given
For souls to be won for the Kingdom of Heaven.
The teaching you give us is all from God's Word
To encourage us to walk in the ways of the Lord.
We love you both, you're simply the best
Your life, your work, may God richly bless.

*The £10 donation*

It was late afternoon, and there were only a few more yards of flooring to be nailed down to finish an area, when Duncan realised that there were no nails left in the box, and worse still no money in the kitty to buy more. As usual, prayer went up to Father God. It would have been good to finish that area of flooring upstairs in the sanctuary that afternoon, in order to enable other work to begin in the morning. At that moment, there was a knocking and a ringing of the doorbell – quite urgently. When Duncan opened it, there stood a good friend, whom we shall call "M", with a story and a £10 note.

When "M" had gone to her church earlier in the day, she was about to put her offering into the collection bowl, when she heard a voice within her telling her to take the money to the man in the church down the road, who was renovating the old church building and had need of it. Our friend "M" duly plucked up courage and arrived late in the afternoon. To her surprise, Duncan told her how he had just been praying to God for some money to enable him to finish the job.

The next day, Duncan called "M" into the church, took her upstairs and both Jim and Duncan showed her where her £10 had helped to finish the job. She was delighted and blessed by being obedient to the still small voice.

There are many occasions such as the above when God heard and answered prayer – too many to record here. 1 Samuel 15:22 says, "*To obey is better than sacrifice*".

## *An 'encounter' by the river*

One day, in April 2001, the weather was gloriously hot, and Duncan had made arrangements to be at the Centre early as two people had promised to come and help him with a particular job. As he waited for them to arrive, a minibus drew up in the car park opposite the church, and a number of Christian people as well as a couple of Pastors boarded the bus and waved goodbye, as off they went on their 'day out'. How lovely, thought Duncan. It would be good to have a day off, but I must be about my Father's business, and carry on with the renovations. He waited and waited and waited for the two men who had promised to come, but there was no sign of them. It was nearly 3 p.m., and the day was almost gone. He had been in the building since 7:30 a.m. Despair and disappointment set in. Do people have no sense of duty, if they vow a vow to God why do they not keep it? If they could not come, why did they not contact him?

As all these things were going through his mind, the enemy

entered, and he became very angry. Why should he bother when no one seemed to care? Almost always, no one even had the initiative to come and brush the floor at the end of the day, when he had finished the finer work. It would have made his life less tiring, and he could have arrived home earlier. All these negative thoughts were going through his mind. Every man minding his own, instead of the Lord's business. That was something he could never understand. What and Who is our first priority? The work of the Lord always came first in his life. It seems there is only a small remnant of dedicated handmaidens and servants left and, as the Word indicates, the love of many would grow cold towards the end of the age.

At that point, Duncan locked up the big, old-fashioned, brown door and in his words, he wanted to "fling the keys into the river and walk away from it all". The afternoon was warm, and the Low Green quiet, as he made his way to one of the benches by the river. After a few minutes, a gentleman in a silver-grey suit and red tie approached, and asked if he could join him. Without hesitation, Duncan said that it was all right. The man said to him, "Your wife's name is Greta". Immediately, Duncan sat up and asked how he knew, because he had never met him before. He replied, "I know a lot about you. The work you are doing is a great work. One day, it will be as a lighthouse. Expect a bright tomorrow, all will be well". Many more words were spoken, which were for his ears alone.

At one point, the man said, "Can we pray?" As he prayed, Duncan told me afterwards, he could feel as it were musical notes stirring from his inmost soul, cleansing and healing his troubled mind. He felt he was rising higher and higher in his spirit, and all the disappointment was being washed away. He felt refreshed and clean. As he looked at the man, (who did not tell him his name when asked) his silver-grey suit and red tie seemed to shimmer in the late afternoon sun. Suddenly, the man said, "Would you pray now?" Duncan began to pray, and then opened his eyes after a few seconds and the man had gone. He was simply nowhere to be seen. There was only one man with a dog in the whole of the Low Green area, and he was quite a bit away. Duncan later told me that he ran towards the man, and asked him, "Did you see a man with a silver-grey suit here a few minutes ago?" The man replied that he had seen no one, and that the Low Green had been practically empty that day.

Feeling a new lease of life, Duncan went back to the church and, once upstairs, he again sensed the presence of the man who had sat beside him on the riverside bench. He believed that God had sent an angel to encourage him in the work and not to give up, because "All was well" as the angel had told him. Strengthened in this knowledge, he set to and made the window seats in the Sanctuary, which fitted perfectly. He felt indeed that "God was with him".

It took Duncan two days to tell me of this experience as he was so overwhelmed by all that had transpired. It certainly encouraged us to go on and not to doubt. I was greatly blessed knowing that the angels knew my name and felt that we had been discussed in the courts of heaven enough for God to send his angel to encourage and exhort us to continue in the work of the Lord in Irvine. Out of this experience, Duncan wrote this song:

> Alone with God, the doors all shut, I see His Face
> I feel His love so strong and true, I know His grace,
> His comfort comes in strength and power to fill my soul,
> Alone with God how blest it is to come apart.

The words kept repeating in Duncan's mind and spirit, until we felt that others would perhaps be blessed if it were written down. In a conversation with a dear friend, Pastor Omri Bowen from Wales, it was decided that Duncan would sing the chorus over the telephone, and Pastor Omri would put it to music, which we are blessed to have today.

Good upholsterers are thin on the ground these days, but we

heard of Ken who came and did a beautiful job covering all of the window seats. He has remained a good friend.

Another person of note was old George, the only plasterer in the whole district who could arch the upstairs windows to Planning Department specifications. Duncan made the moulds, nailed them into place, and George completed the plastering. Looking at them today, one would think that they had been there since the beginning of time.

Many came to help in the years of renovation, and our thanks go out to every one for their invaluable contribution to restoring this fine building for the praise and glory of His Name.

*The right hand of fellowship into membership*

At that time, Duncan was preparing to be accepted into the Fellowship of a large Glasgow Church. One Saturday, the two of us were sitting in the living room of my mother's house in Larbert having a time of prayer, when suddenly Duncan fell to the floor and stayed there. Mother and Auntie Mary came rushing in. We wondered what had happened. Was he ill, had he taken a fit, what was wrong?

Eventually, after a few minutes, he rose to his feet and told us that an angel had appeared to him carrying a large cross, which he handed to Duncan, saying that God would bless him and that God had His hand of anointing upon him, but it would be a cross-life, and there would be many battles.

God is wise when He hides the future from us. If we knew what was ahead, we would opt out of our high and holy calling many a time, but we would have a lifetime of regrets. A day at a time is God's motto.

## *Israel – God's land*

I had been to Israel in 1995, and I yearned to go back. After a particularly blessed cameo evening, I asked around, "If I were to go to Israel, who would come with me?" A good number really felt in their heart that they would love to visit the Holy Land. I will never forget the day when twelve sisters boarded the mini-bus, waved cheerio to friends, and off we went to the airport, bound for Tel Aviv's Ben Gurion Airport. It was excitement by the ton all the way!

I had heard through the grapevine that the House of Peace in Jerusalem was quite small and that it might not suit us. However, when we arrived, all doubts and fears were dispelled, and we fell in love with the marble floors, open staircase, and wonderful hospitality of the people there. Patricia and Caroline could not do enough for us. They made everyone welcome, and immediately we felt at home.

How we loved to watch the first three stars appear in the inky black eastern sky in the evening. This signifies the start of a new day. We enjoyed our very first Shabbat meal on the Friday night, and then we sang and danced the night away adorned in our best frocks. Golgotha, the tomb, and the garden are all amazing sights to those who have never visited before. We shared communion together and sang songs of praise and worship to the King of Kings and Lord of Lords.

There is so much to see and so many places to visit, and although it was exhilarating, it was also, at times, exhausting. Even though it was November, the weather was very hot, and certainly not what we are used to in Scotland! Towards the end of the twelve-day tour, I received a telephone call from Duncan saying that he had not been too well, and was looking forward to me coming home. I was a bit alarmed, because he never admitted to being unwell, and so I was rather anxious to return home to see what the problem was.

Usually, he would wait at the end of the path with a big smile, and carry our bags into the house. Then there would be hugs all round, and cups of tea, as we talked of our adventures. Instead, he was sitting in his chair by the fireside, pale and looking drawn. His first words were, "Greta, I haven't slept much since you left home. My back has been so sore. I've been to the doctor, but it has not helped". Before we left, there had been little indication that he was unwell.

I swung into action at once, and telephoned a chiropractor for an appointment to see if she could pinpoint the problem. Duncan had been to the local hospital, to see if they could give him an x-ray one evening, but they were so busy that they could not take him for five hours. He came home instead of waiting all that time.

Initially, he felt some relief from the chiropractor's consultations, but eventually, it was back to square one. Christmas and New Year passed, and we were due to go to Ireland for a few days' break One night, the pain was so bad that Pastor Bridie prayed with him practically the whole night. It was touch and go whether she would take him to the hospital, but Duncan declined, as he was so tired. He finally fell asleep exhausted, and slept until the morning.

During this time, he would still go down to the Centre and work, but all the time not knowing what was really wrong. One day, I took things into my own hands, because we were not getting much sleep, and I felt this must be addressed as the pain was not going away, and prayer was made for him day and night.

We went to the surgery, where there was a locum doctor on call, and Duncan explained about the severe pain in his back. Immediately, the doctor suggested having an x-ray, and we were at the hospital within half an hour!

The next day, Duncan came home from the Centre early, and said that he was going upstairs to have a rest. I went out for a few minutes, and during that time, the telephone rang in the bedroom. It was the doctor from the surgery. He told Duncan that he had the results of the x-ray, but that the prognosis was not good. It was bone cancer and Duncan would need to come back to the surgery to make arrangements for the treatment.

We cannot fathom the ways and mind of God when things go wrong. You know that you are doing what He has asked you to do, and so we felt that we just had to trust Him. There was nowhere else to turn, but to the fountain of living waters.

Arrangements were quickly made for Duncan to be treated by one of the finest oncologists in Glasgow. For months from March to October 2003, we travelled to and from the Hospital where he underwent radiotherapy. Occasionally, he had to stay there for a few days.

One incident stands out in my mind particularly. He had to have chemotherapy in the local hospital that week, and so, on this particular day, his treatment was started rather late in the afternoon. I thought, "Tonight, I'll get a good night's sleep. He'll be well looked after in the hospital". I was warmly tucked up in bed when the telephone rang at 11:30 p.m. "Can you come for me? I am allowed home tonight". Of course, my tiredness disappeared, and I was off like a shot.

The purpose of mentioning this episode is that there is a very strange feeling walking through dimly lit hospital corridors at midnight, entering a lift on your own, and meeting no one. Not even a doctor or a cleaner. The eeriness is hard to describe. It is so different throughout the day, bustle and chatter everywhere, but beyond midnight is another story. When I arrived at the ward entrance, there he was, stick and all, waiting for me; the relief on his face said it all, it was worth the effort.

Most of Duncan's treatment was in the Beatson Hospital in Glasgow where Robin, his brother, worked at that time, but he would not hear of anybody driving him up to Glasgow except me. At times, I had to cry to God to give me energy and heighten my perception while driving and pray the angels round about the car. It was good either before or after treatment to have a cup of tea with Robin and talk about various topics.

It was round about this time that Duncan and I had the great pleasure of knowing that Robin and his family had come back to the Lord, and that they were wondering which church to attend. It seemed right to point them in the direction of 'The Victory Centre Church', which at that time, met in the Assembly Hall of Allan Glen's school, Glasgow. They felt very much at home there, as formerly Shenner, Duncan and Robin's dad, had worked there as a teacher for many years. They had both visited the school on many occasions for bagpipe competitions, or sports days.

Months passed since that portentous afternoon in February 2003, when the news of cancer exploded into our lives, shattering our dreams. Does God heal? Would He heal? Many people were praying that God would heal suddenly and unexpectedly, and great glory would come to His Name!

## *Holiday at Port Appin*

The October school holidays came quickly that year and we decided go to the log cabin for a week with Robin, Sandra and the two girls. The drive via Oban was uneventful. We stopped for coffee at Inveraray, and another break to stretch our legs and breathe in the fresh mountain air.

The nurses who attended Duncan were absolutely wonderful and encouraged us to have a little break. They also made sure that we had plenty of medication and an emergency contact telephone number. We were happy to be packing once more for pleasure and not for hospital.

We had never been to the cabin before, so when we drove up the bush-lined driveway and turned the corner into the car park, we were greatly delighted to find a rather large, ranch-type cabin house with a separate annexe totally self-sufficient, which was to be our little house for the week. We were thrilled, especially with the view of Loch Linnhe, which flowed into the Firth of Lorn with sailing boats cruising up and down the narrow stretch of water.

The weather was fine and dry most mornings, and so we took advantage of the sunshine and enjoyed breakfast with the family on the open decking. Because it was the school holidays, our son Gillies, wife Celia, Ross and Jack drove over from Aberdeen to join us for a day, staying overnight in a local hotel. It was to be the very last holiday that we would have together.

We played 'snap' and different card games, enjoyed chatting round the log fire in the evening, taking photographs, and eating good food – we especially enjoyed the hot chocolate all frothed up before retiring for the night. Life seemed to be enjoyable once more with all the family round about us. Their love and attention comforted us and made the dark clouds roll away for a few hours.

With the help of a wheelchair, we managed to go to Oban for the day and have a browse round the shops, which Duncan enjoyed immensely. Tanya and Lara picked up a few bargains on the way, had ice cream and the usual sweets. We had café lattes and buttered scones and watched the boats leave for the islands of Mull, Jura, Islay, and the islands further afield. All the time, the seagulls were screeching overhead looking for crumbs from the tourists.

The week was passing all too quickly. On the Thursday night, Duncan's pain was really very severe, and he could not get to sleep no matter which way he turned or sat up. We cried to God to help, and finally, he managed to lie down for a few hours. I decided that we should go home a day early, and alerted the McMillan nurses to attend him when we arrived back.

We said our goodbyes to the family, and I drove the little red Corsa back home to Irvine with only one stop at Inveraray. Duncan really was very sick. Like all good times, it was good to get away and good to get home again to the old familiar things and the usual comforts we take for granted, plus the wonderful supportive help of the nurses from the local surgery.

All this time, we were being upheld by the prayers of the saints, and we never faltered in our faith that God could intervene at any given moment of time. One friend wrote out 31 healing scriptures on card, one for every day in the month to cling to and pray back to God.

### *A Saturday afternoon*

Two weeks after the short holiday to Port Appin and two weeks before Duncan went to be with the Lord, I came home from shopping one really cold wet miserable Saturday afternoon towards the end of October, with five bags of heavy groceries and unloaded them on to the kitchen worktop. I had only been in a minute, when Duncan put the kettle on for a cup of tea, and said that he wanted to talk to me. I thought, this sounds like serious business, I do not know if I am going to like this!

With mugs of tea on the table, the conversation began. "Greta, the Lord is taking me home, and, as you have the vision for the Centre, He wants you to carry on the work!" Well, explosion on my part was the understatement of the year. My reply went something like this: If God does not heal you, there is no way I am even going to be a Christian, far less put my foot in the door of the Emmanuel Christian Centre, that's it finished. How can I possibly carry on the work myself? We were called together to pioneer and pastor the work, and that it would be cruel of God to do this, when the Centre could be opened next year (2004). My dreams, aspirations and vision totally disintegrated at that moment.

I had not reckoned on God. Duncan spoke again when I had re-arranged my thinking. “Greta, you got the vision for the work all those years ago. My time here is finished. I have done what the Lord asked me to do, and I must submit to His will. You are strong in the Lord and anointed. You have known the Saviour from a child, and God will be with you. Always do what is in your heart, and do not seek man’s opinions. If the Team in the Centre are with you and support you in every way, carry on, but if not, or you feel pressurised and lack help, there is always Plan B”.

I have hidden Plan B in my heart, but there has been no need to resort to it because the Team Members have been the best, most supportive, and I have lacked nothing. Christ Jesus is my best Friend at all times, loyal and true.

When I have needed wisdom, I have had to run to the secret place of the Most High and nestle under the shadow of His wings. At other times, I have asked counsel of the Spirit-led friends with whom He has surrounded me. I am so blessed to have wonderful confidantes I can turn to at any time. Being affiliated with New Testament Ministries International, Rev Peter Scothern being the Director, I draw on Brother Peter’s wise counsel from time to time, and value his discernment in matters both natural and spiritual.

*The parting of the ways*

At the time, I did not realise it, but my life and my future changed forever, after the conversation that Duncan and I had on that memorable, wet Saturday afternoon. I still hung on in the hope that even at the last minute the Lord could intervene with

His Mighty Healing Power and touch my clever, wise, husband.

Busy days passed with people coming and going. Our very supportive daughter Elaine took one week's unpaid leave every month for nine months, in order to help me care for her Dad. Duncan's face would light up when the telephone rang, and I would tell him that Elaine was coming the next week. They had a special relationship, which some daughters have with their father, and it was good for her to hide in her heart the special times they spent together. Multitudes of others who have gone through the same trauma of nursing family members with cancer or other serious life threatening diseases will identify with the relief it is to have someone share the burden.

The days slipped by with nurses coming and going – beautiful girls, gentle and kind in every way Whenever the telephone rang, the same story would be told every time, "All is well. Duncan is in the hands of the Lord. Please pray for the pain to be less severe at night so that he can have a good rest". Always, he would say, "Oh, for the dawning to come, then I can sleep"

Elaine was due to come on 17th November, but when she telephoned, we both said at the same time, "Can you not make it the 10th?" For some reason, we both felt the 17th was too far away and it would be lovely to have her with us sooner. Duncan was getting weaker, and I was very tired with the constant burden of caring. Make no mistake about anything, we are all human beings together, and at the end of the day just made of dust as the good Book says. You think your loved one is going to last until at least Christmas, and then we will see how it goes from there!

I ministered at the service as usual on the last Sunday morning. Wendy came to the house and sat with Duncan. What a blessing those precious people were at that time. After tea that Sunday evening of 9th November 2003, Duncan said, "Don't go to the meeting tonight. Stay with me Greta and keep me company, and get ready for Elaine coming tomorrow". We sat down to watch

'Songs of Praise' and within five minutes, Duncan was sleeping.

I now know that Duncan was aware that he was nearing the time when the Lord was going to take him home. There was a quietness in the house, not an eerie stillness, but a hush as the angels came ready to take his spirit to the Lord Jesus in Heaven. The atmosphere changed slightly, and I found we were walking about quieter, and amazingly, the telephone did not ring so often.

Elaine arrived on Monday evening, the 10th November with gifts and lots of help and love. She immediately took over the responsibility, and I could sigh with relief. We were offered the help of night nurses, but Duncan, like many men, was a very private person and just wanted his own round about him.

The next morning, Tuesday 11th, the day nurses took me into the kitchen and told me the end was near. Somehow, I just could not believe this or take it in. All of you reading this, who have experienced a 'valley of Baca', will understand and know what I mean. One goes through the motions. We try to sing and keep busy, then the doorbell rings, more nurses or doctors, medication, this changed, that other thing put in place, it goes on relentlessly. Anyone for coffee?

By Tuesday night, Elaine and I were very tired. The doorbell rang again, and in walked Mary, Allyson and Margaret, making a quick detour to Irvine to visit Duncan on their way to England, but they had to leave by about 8 o'clock. Quick cups of tea all round and Duncan brightened up with the banter of the unexpected company. Ten o'clock came, then midnight. The guests were still here! I made beds all over the house. It was good sharing the long hours of the night, and we took it in turns to be vigilant towards our precious cargo.

Mornings are very welcoming, and it was lovely to see the dawn of another new day. Our friends went on their way having stayed and talked and laughed, stirring up memories of good days gone by. Duncan enjoyed the surprise visit, and appreciated the fact that they gave their support to Elaine and me.

It was time to telephone the family to come as soon as they could. Robin and Sandra got time off work and hurried down to Irvine. Time was running out, and we just wanted to be at Duncan's side, hold hands, and talk quietly. Finally, Duncan turned to me and said, "Greta, everything you have done for me has been like little rosebuds of love, thank you". After a short time of resting, he asked for a spoonful of lemon mousse to taste his mouth and was satisfied.

Robin nipped upstairs for a few minutes, and Sandra had just gone into the kitchen with the tray of cups, when our precious one turned to Elaine and me, as we were holding his now soft hands and said "Greta, Elaine", and he went into the presence of the Saviour that minute.

All was peace and all was rest at 12:50 p.m. that Wednesday afternoon of 12th November. Free from pain and this old world's cares, "*absent from the body, present with the Lord*". How reassuring to know, at the end of the day, that your faith is in Almighty God. As Job could say, "*The Lord gives and the Lord takes, blessed be the name of the Lord*".

Our son Gillies was wonderful as he undertook all the funeral arrangements. He had travelled down from Aberdeen, and it left Elaine and me free to do the other necessary things. God puts people in families to help in times of trouble and need as well as the joyful occasions. That is why He came to earth to set up His Kingdom, so that we might have sweet fellowship with His wonderful people (some of us He is still working on!), to come together to worship and praise, study His unerring Word, and pray for others to be spiritually renewed in Christ Jesus just as He planned, by going to the cross of Calvary over 2,000 years ago, so that we could know the joy of sins forgiven.

Many people braved the very wet day and attended the Funeral Service, which was held in the Old Parish Church in Irvine, kindly loaned to us. We saw old friends, new friends, neighbours, acquaintances, as well as near family, cousins, and church people from different denominations. Some guests travelled a long distance to pay their respects. They were all very welcome to share in our common grief for a well-loved husband, father and friend, pastor-pioneer and confidant. Maldwyn Edwards was the presiding minister at the service, with others participating and sharing their love and respect. The family and I were comforted at the gracious words spoken.

# Chapter Four

## And afterwards

The days passed and everybody had gone home, back to their own respective area of living and working. All who have walked this way before me know of the abject, awful, aloneness of this journey. There are daily reminders of the way things 'used to be', and having to put the key in the door to emptiness.

Having faith in the Living God makes all the difference. He brings sunshine into life as you begin to live again. Fellowship and true friends are there when needed, without intrusion. The Bible says, "The Lord would be a husband to the widow". He has been that and more besides; He has raised up people to support and comfort when needed. One cannot empathise with others unless you have walked the same road.

On a glorious morning, in the not too distant future, we will all meet around the Throne in Glory to worship the King of Kings and Lord of all Lords, whose Name is Jesus Christ, the same yesterday, today and forever! For those who have not made the decision to follow the best Friend and Saviour you could ever have, do it today and you will know peace and joy in your heart. Otherwise, you will face eternity alone and without hope when your turn comes to meet the Master, as it surely will.

*The first Christmas*

- *Glory to God in the highest, and on earth peace, goodwill towards men (Luke 2:14).*

This must pass, as it is too painful to put into words. Some will understand, others just do not know or comprehend the poverty of spirit as cards came thundering through the letter box that first Christmas with lavish words of 'have a wonderful Christmas

Season' when the heart is crushed and breaking. Simply to write a few cards to a small number of far-off friends with only one name on the brightly coloured card instead of the usual two takes every ounce of determination to overcome and not feel sorry for oneself, but to resolutely live for tomorrow and have a dream.

One looks at the lone name and thoughts fly off like sparks from a million-coloured fireworks! This is final, things will never, ever be the same – this is really for real! "Start and get your act together and with God you can make it". He says in His Word that He will never leave us nor forsake us. Begin to make a difference. Think of others who really have no hope and be thankful for what you have left; do not dwell on what you have lost. We, who are attached to Him, have a glorious future, so it is up to us to share the love of Jesus with others and tell them what a difference He makes in our life.

*Life after new year 2003*

- *Give, (of yourself) and it shall be given back to you, good measure, pressed down, shaken together, and running over (Luke 6:38).*

It was now time to turn the losses around, to look at what I had left, and begin to bring things together. If ever we need someone to tell us how to turn things around, go to God. He is an expert on the subject, because He suffered more loss than anyone who has ever lived. Our Christ was human as well as Divine, and He left the splendours of heaven and constant fellowship with the Father and the Holy Spirit, to come down to earth to redeem us back to God by His precious blood shed on the cross of Calvary.

It was also time to reassess the work still to be completed in the West Road Church building. Thankfully, the bulk of the work had been finished, but many finishing touches had to be attended to, such as tiles for the vestibule, office furniture, invalid toilet with the extras that entails. Carpets to be laid upstairs, a huge undertaking, especially when the carpet fitters do not turn up when promised. Nevertheless, I was not alone by any means. Interested parties came to help and offer advice. Also, the Team Members were keen to see the Centre finished and to begin participating in the vision that the Lord had given so many years before.

Because Duncan and I had worked hand-in-hand, I just slipped into the role quite naturally of ordering materials, hiring men, (and sometimes firing when the job was not being done properly), moving from one challenge to the next, and gaining ground week by week. If anybody needs to get over grief quickly, immerse yourself in hard work during the day and sleep will soon overtake you at night.

The question was put to me more than a few times, “When is the Centre going to be opened?” I really did not know. I had to consult the Holy Spirit who had promised to lead and guide me into all truth. One fine morning, in April 2004, I awoke feeling good, and I just knew that a date had to be arrived at, and an invitation list drawn up. What a mammoth task – which names to include and which to consider. There were so many people interested in coming, in order to help share in our joy and to see what God had done. Lists had to be drawn up.

The wrong tiles for the entrance had been delivered – just one of the many setbacks that Spring. The ‘plumber’, who had marital problems, decided not to come back, and so another had to finish a rather bad job. It certainly was interesting; life was never dull. The carpet fitters – well that is another story!

The Opening Day was to be the 5th June 2004. This day would also incorporate a Memorial Service for Duncan as Co-pioneer and Pastor of the Emmanuel Christian Centre.

What to do about chairs for the people to sit on? We only had £300 in the Bank, but we still had great faith in the Lord, who had called us, and we knew that He would remain faithful to the end. We had heard about a good warehouse in Dumbarton, and so, one morning, needing at least 200 chairs for the upstairs sanctuary, we set off for that warehouse with a song in our heart. We already had been given a number of blue velvet chairs for the multi-purpose area downstairs; however, pink velvet with gold round about was the favourite colour for upstairs.

We must have viewed every kind of chair that the warehouse had in stock, but we could not make up our minds as to which ones we really wanted. Suddenly, away up high, someone spotted two or three pink chairs with gold legs. We immediately drew the attention of the manager to this, and they were brought down for examination. How much would 200 plus, pink chairs cost? We were soon told the price – £3,400, and they had to be paid for on arrival in two weeks' time!

Faith always prevails and says it can be done, so we agreed the contract. We thanked the Lord all the way home for undertaking thus far as well as for the rest of the money to come in to pay the bill. We told the Lord that if we needed a chair in our own house, we would go out and buy it. Surely, He could meet the cost of 200 chairs for His House so that the people could sit down at the great Opening Day in two weeks' time, because this House "*was the Lord's doing and it was marvellous in our eyes*" (Psalm 118:23).

The cost of the chairs was mentioned in the morning Service, but not unduly advertised. As was our custom, we prayed as a Team, trusted God, and thanked Him for His great provision, and true to His Divine Nature, the price of the 210 chairs was in the kitty when they were delivered, three days before the official opening! "What a great God you have". "You must have some faith", were some of the comments. But, we reminded the people what the Word of God says in Hebrews 11:6, "*Without faith it is impossible to please Him, for he that comes to God must believe that He is, and that He is a rewarder of those who diligently seek*

*Him*".

What a joy to see lovely new pink chairs being delivered and brought into the renovated upstairs sanctuary. I thought, "If only Duncan could see this wondrous sight". It may not seem a great thing to many people, but I looked back to the day, when approximately thirty people stood on a dirty, dark, dingy gallery and said, "We'll agree with you (Duncan and Greta) to take this building, and we will be behind you all the way". Now that the chairs were finally being put into place on top of the biscuit-coloured 100% pure wool carpet, I thought, "To God be all the glory in Emmanuel's land". I hope the dear Lord somehow let Duncan know that we made it, and it is a beautiful sight to behold. Today, people walk in there every weekend, and never give it a thought, but to us who walked the way of faith we see miracles everywhere we look!

*The great opening day – 5th June 2004*

Questions flooded my mind night after night. With no immediate right-hand pastor to consult, I hoped everything that could be done had been done. Cards printed, lists drawn up – too many for the Opening Day, there would have to be another 'Open Day' two-weeks later to enable the overflow of interested parties to come and share in our joy. This done I could rest somewhat. The Team Members were most supportive and their help was invaluable at this very important and emotive time for me personally.

The day dawned bright and clear, and the new Emmanuel Christian Centre was duly opened by our local MSP, Mrs Irene Oldfather at 2.45 p.m., to the skirl of the pipes playing "Amazing Grace" among other stirring melodies.

A gold plated plaque was unveiled at the top of the wide sweeping staircase by our life-long friend Mary. Then it was into the upstairs Sanctuary to thank God Almighty for His goodness and mercy to us over the years, and for bringing us to this occasion at this time. As I looked down on those who had congregated, I was exceptionally proud to have my son and daughter, nieces, cousins and other relatives from far and near, especially Duncan's cousin Mima from Tomintoul, as they were brought up together and loved going to their Granny's to be spoiled at the weekends. So many people, precious friends, associates in the work of the Lord, 'singers' from the British Legion, neighbours, some who had worked to beautify the House of the Lord, Pastors and Ministers, all gathered to glorify what the Lord done in Irvine.

The afternoon session incorporated a Memorial Service for Duncan as co-pioneer and co-pastor of the work. Many people paid tribute and some, because of time, had to sit with their notes unread. The loss is great, we miss his cheery smiling face, and in my quieter moments, I wonder sometimes what it is all about. Then I remember Duncan's words to me: "You received the vision; you hear from God; He has anointed you to carry on the work. The Lord has told me my time on earth is over now. I've done what He asked me to do". So in that, I have to be content until the good Lord reveals His further will and plan for my life.

Rev Peter Scothern flew up to Scotland to speak at the Open Day celebration, and a wonderful weekend ensued. Brother Peter has such insight into end-time things, and we have found his ministry quite remarkable. As we are under the canopy of New Testament Ministries, it was especially good for us to have the Director with us on that occasion, and we were all greatly blessed and still remember his words to us.

*God's work goes on*

Duncan had a saying, "God buries his workmen, but His work goes on". It was hard to think that he was not with us at the beginning of the work in the newly renovated and refurbished Emmanuel Christian Centre. It was with heavy hearts that we left the old Perceton country church to begin worshipping in the town centre again, but we gained strength and the vision returned as the days and weeks progressed.

Personally, I wondered how things would ‘pan out’ when I alone was the ‘pastor’. Would the Team stay with me, stand by me, support me, or gradually move on to pastures new? Thankfully, almost all are standing shoulder to shoulder with me in the work of the Lord, and it has been so marvellously encouraging to look on and observe how God the Holy Spirit has matured and beautified His people in the midst of much affliction, upheaval and walk of faith.

If there was a special need that called for sacrificial giving, then members, friends, both far and near who were interested in the on-going work, were there praying, fasting, believing and giving out of their own pocket. What joy followed, as the obedience saw a great need met, as we learned the lesson a long time ago, “If you will, I will”, as He is faithful who calls.

We cannot have a harvest if we do not first sow a seed. Just like the farmer, if he keeps his seed in a sack in the barn, when he goes out to the field and looks for the first green shoots to appear like the other farmers, he will be sadly disappointed. He has nothing because his seed is still in the barn. What a waste! Make sure that you plant your seed into good soil so that when harvest-time comes, you also will reap plentifully.

## *Seven-days-a-week ministry*

It takes time to get structures established and everything does not always fall into place overnight. At this moment, some four years after the Opening Day, the ministries that God entrusted to us are being established: women’s work, men’s ministry, children’s church, mothers’ and toddlers’ group, puppet group, and the coffee shop (open five mornings a week for tea, coffee, toast and marmalade, home made scones, etc.).

One area of ministry that had been our vision since the Centre began in August 1983 has been the Bible School, which commenced in September 2007. Jennifer Muir from America is a tremendous Facilitator for the School, and has done a wonderful job faithfully every Saturday in encouraging the students, marking exam papers, and all that goes with a vibrant Bible School. We recommend the 'International School of Ministry' to any prospective student – it is most comprehensive and spiritually enlightening.

The 25th Anniversary of the Emmanuel Christian Centre in Irvine came and went remarkably quickly. The old adage is so very true, 'Time and tide wait for no man'. The years have galloped on; there have been many changes of various kinds, but our God remains constant and is the same 'Yesterday, today and forever'

The Graduation Service for ten students was held on Saturday 7th June 2008 during the celebrations for the 25th anniversary. In the 'Emmanuel', as it is affectionately known, there is always something good and exciting to look forward to and this was one of those weekends. Professor Roy Peacock was the main speaker during this weekend. Two greatly anointed ladies from California, USA came to be with us at that time to officiate at the Graduation Service.

Recently, we have just returned from a wonderful three days of holy convocation in the lovely Seamill Hydro Hotel – good fellowship, good fun and the best of cuisine! The Lord came in His mighty power and love and filled the place with His glory where we were sitting. These are powerful days, days prior to the soon return of the Lord Jesus Christ for His Bride. We must go on; there is no time to look back. As we heard at the Conference from 1 Samuel 16:1, "Are you a yesterday's man (Saul), a today's man (Samuel), or a tomorrow's man (David)?" There is great food for thought hidden in that scripture.

*Do no uncommanded work*
*(only do what he tells you to do)*

One piercing word, which I brought back in my spirit from my journeyings in Jerusalem this January 2008, was this: "Do no uncommanded work". We can be too busy being busy, when the Lord wants us to "*Be still and know that I am God*" (Psalm 46:10). He is looking for a balanced people in these days of rushing here and there trying to meet deadlines. Let us have an ear to hear what the Spirit is saying to the church, and get our priorities in Divine order.

***The following Word from the Lord came through a visiting Prophet approximately 3 years ago:***

*"Pastor Greta, Man has not called you, I have called you I have a work for you to do and I want to touch My people at this time. I have called you because you have an obedient spirit and I can trust you. Do not fear man, the fear of man is a snare - be obedient. I have many places to take you and you will speak of the things you have been through. You already know that I will meet your every need. You have proved Me in this, and you will prove Me again. I will ask you to do things and the finances won't be there, but as you go forward in faith and trust in Me you will prove Me again in this, for I am your God who supplies every need. The smile of My face is upon you, My anointing is upon you. I have a future for you, for your good. Man has not called you, I have called you, I have called you."*

## *Pastor Duncan – 1996*

*I know a man, a Godly man – my Pastor*
*Who works by faith the way of the Master*
*Who all through the day seeks His face*
*And in all he does sings God's praise*

*He is a man who has a vision*
*He is a man on a mission*
*To complete the work the Lord has given*
*He is a man who won't stand still*
*Ever eager and ready to do God's will*

*With the faithful few by his side*
*He toils all day 'till eventide*
*Only God alone hears his weary sighs*
*And hears his silent cries*

*Tirelessly working he gives his all*
*Thinking of others, himself least of all*
*He has a heart like a lion, fearless and strong*
*Yet so gentle and full of love for everyone.*

*Ann A*